IN VISIBLE
FELLOWSHIP

In Visible Fellowship

❦

A CONTEMPORARY VIEW OF
BONHOEFFER'S CLASSIC WORK
LIFE TOGETHER

JON WALKER

LEAFWOOD
PUBLISHERS

IN VISIBLE FELLOWSHIP

A Contemporary View of Bonhoeffer's Classic Work Life Together

Copyright 2011 by Jon Walker

ISBN 978-0-89112-295-1

Printed in the United States of America

Numerous brief excerpts from *Life Togeth*er by Dietrich Bonhoeffer and translated by John Doberstein. English translation copyright 1954 by Harper & Brothers, copyright renewed 1982 by Helen S. Doberstein. Reprinted by permission of HarperCollins Publishers.

Scripture quotations, unless otherwise noted, are from The Holy Bible, New International Version. Copyright 1984, International Bible Society. Used by permission of Zondervan Publishers.

Cover design by Thinkpen Design, Inc.
Interior text design by Sandy Armstrong

Leafwood Publishers
1626 Campus Court
Abilene, Texas 79601
1-877-816-4455 toll free

For current information about all Leafwood titles, visit our Web site:
www.leafwoodpublishers.com

11 12 13 14 15 16 / 7 6 5 4 3 2 1

To Lori Hensley, who exemplifies these biblical truths in a remarkable way. I am blessed to follow in your footsteps as we follow after Jesus.

Acknowledgements

It is impossible to write a book without admitting, like Tennyson, "I am part of all that I have met." That being the case, it is beyond my abilities to thank everyone who helped me while writing this manuscript, but I do want to mention contributions by David and Susan Moffitt, Kathy Chapman Sharp, Doug Hart, Doug Slaybaugh, Grace Guthrie, Kelly J. Sims, Mark Kelly, Tobin Perry, David Chrzan, Brandon Cox, Steve Pettit, Rick Warren, Judy Black, Bucky Rosenbaum, Gary Myers, Leonard Allen, Terry Utley, Christopher Walker, Nathan Walker, and Jasmine.

CONTENTS

Bonhoeffer Biography 9

Introduction 13

Chapter 1   We Were Created to Live in
             Visible Christian Fellowship 15

Chapter 2   We Were Created to Share God's Grace Together 21

Chapter 3   We Were Created for the Life of Jesus to
             Live Inside Us 25

Chapter 4   We Were Created to Live in the Reality of
             Christian Community 29

Chapter 5   We Were Created to Learn How to Love in Christ-
             community 35

Chapter 6   The Day's Beginning: Morning Praise 41

Chapter 7   The Day's Beginning: Praying the Psalms 47

Chapter 8   The Day's Beginning: God's Word 51

Chapter 9   The Day's Beginning: Singing the New Song 57

Chapter 10   The Day's Beginning: Saying Our Prayers Together 63

Chapter 11   The Day's Beginning: The Fellowship of the Table 69

Chapter 12   The Day's Work 73

Chapter 13   Mid-day Worship 77

Chapter 14   Evening Worship 81

Chapter 15   The Day Alone: When Loneliness
             Misuses Community 85

Chapter 16   The Day Alone: Solitude and Silence 89

Chapter 17   The Day Alone: Meditation 93

Chapter 18   The Day Alone: Prayer 97

Chapter 19   The Day Alone: Intercession 101

Chapter 20   The Test of Meditation 105

Chapter 21   Ranking Rivals While Ignoring God 109

Chapter 22   The Ministry of Speaking the Truth in Love 113

Chapter 23 The Ministry of Meekness 117

Chapter 24 The Ministry of Listening 121

Chapter 25 The Ministry of Helpfulness..125

Chapter 26 The Ministry of Bearing 129

Chapter 27 The Ministry of Proclaiming 133

Chapter 28 The Ministry of Authority...139

Chapter 29 The Ministry of Confession and Communion 143

Chapter 30 In Confession We Break Through
to the Community..147

Chapter 31 In Confession We Break Through to the Cross............151

Chapter 32 In Confession We Break Through to New Life 155

Chapter 33 In Confession We Break Through to Certainty............159

Chapter 34 Confession: To Whom Do We Confess?.........................163

Chapter 35 Confession: Two Dangers to Avoid....................................167

Chapter 36 The Ministry of Communion 171

DIETRICH BONHOEFFER

Dietrich Bonhoeffer's life was one of risk, where he faced constant choices that required him to take a stand, often putting everything he had—even his life—on the line for what he believed. It's easy to marvel at the way he faced off against Adolf Hitler and the Nazi regime, but in books such as *The Cost of Discipleship*, Bonhoeffer teaches that a life of such extraordinary risk is the *expectation*, not the exception, for any disciple of Jesus.

To me, what is appealing about Bonhoeffer is his authenticity. He walked steadily toward an uncompromising faith in Jesus, and he did it in the difficult and dangerous reality of life, where obeying the commands of Christ can often be heart-wrenching and costly. Perhaps because he was thrust so quickly and so young into life-or-death matters, Bonhoeffer did not play games with pastoral piety or write from an ivory tower.

Too young to be ordained when he first graduated from seminary, Bonhoeffer continued his theological studies at Union Theological Seminary in New York City and for a brief time taught Sunday school at Abyssinian Baptist Church in Harlem, New York. There Adam Clayton Powell, Sr. preached a social gospel that would significantly influence the Civil Rights Movement in the United States.

It was Powell who first used the term "cheap grace" to describe the way the church compromises the gospel when it down-plays the cross and repentance in order to sell an easy discipleship that requires little commitment and suggests there is a pain-free path to heaven. The take-away for Bonhoeffer was that, to echo his own words, his religious phraseology quickly transformed into real Christian action. For such a time as this, God sent him back to Germany.

It was a little over a year after Bonhoeffer was ordained as a Lutheran pastor when the Nazis came to power on January 30, 1933. Bonhoeffer, still only twenty-six-years-old, delivered a radio address two days later, where he warned the German people they were being seduced by the Führer and that their worship of him would lead to idolatry. His broadcast was cut off in mid-sentence.

The young pastor watched in dismay as the state-sponsored church of Germany compromised with Hitler; as a result he became a founding member of the Confessing Church, which was comprised of congregations independent of government sponsorship. A gifted theologian, Bonhoeffer might have taught in any number of professorships or pastorates, but his opposition to Adolf Hitler closed the door to those opportunities. Instead, he began teaching in less formal settings, such as the unofficial Finkenwalde Seminary.

It was at Finkenwalde that Bonhoeffer began writing *The Cost of Discipleship*. He published manuscript in 1937, about the same time the Gestapo shut down the seminary and arrested many of its students. He followed up with his book about Christian community, *Life Together*.

In 1939 Bonhoeffer returned to Union Theological Seminary in New York City to teach, but almost immediately regretted his decision, believing he would have no right to participate in the reconstruction of Christian life in Germany after the war if he wasn't there to share in the hardships of the German people during the war.

Returning to Germany, Bonhoeffer joined the *Abwehr*, a branch of Germany's military intelligence, but also the center for the resistance movement in Germany. For instance, the *Abwehr* worked to undermine Nazi policy toward the Jews, and Bonhoeffer also used his position as cover as he traveled and spoke, something he would not otherwise have been allowed to do.

Bonhoeffer was a pacifist, but he struggled over the moral responsibility of believers to oppose evil when it is incarnate in a government, such as Hitler's Nazi Germany. Could that opposition include the use of violent force? We are always responsible for our moral choices, he said, but if we misunderstand God's direction at such a pivotal moment, Bonhoeffer believed we can fall upon the grace of God.

As a result, he became involved in the plot to assassinate Hitler—not in planning the details, but by attempting to establish communication with England in order to negotiate peace once the Führer was dead.

In April 1943, Bonhoeffer was arrested, essentially for preaching the gospel. He was imprisoned in Tegel military prison while awaiting trial but continued his ministry by writing letters and papers that became a book published posthumously.

It wasn't until after the failed "Valkyrie" assassination attempt on July 20, 1944, that the Gestapo discovered Bonhoeffer's involvement. Hilter ordered his death, and on April 8, 1945, Bonhoeffer was executed by hanging at Flossenbürg concentration camp—a mere three weeks before Hitler committed suicide as the Allies swept into Berlin.

Bonhoeffer died in the same way he lived—focused exclusively on Christ and humbly submitting to the ultimate cost of discipleship. Offered an opportunity to escape, he declined, not wanting to put his family in danger. He was led to the gallows after concluding a Sunday morning service, saying: "This is the end—for me the beginning of life."

He has become one of the most influential theological voices of the twentieth century and *The Cost of Discipleship* is considered a classic in ecclesiological literature. Many of its concepts are now deeply ingrained in modern Protestant thought and practice. His follow-up book to *Discipleship* was *Life Together*.

If you'd like to read more about Bonhoeffer, this excellent biography is available: *Bonhoeffer: Pastor, Martyr, Prophet, Spy*, by Eric Metaxas (Thomas Nelson, 2010).

INTRODUCTION

After Dietrich Bonhoeffer finished writing *Discipleship*, he said he would have changed a few things; for instance, he would have taught that obedience to the commands of Christ must take place within the context of Christian community. In *Discipleship*, Bonhoeffer spoke in terms of immediate, unquestioning obedience to Jesus, but as he watched the Nazis abuse their power, he realized the admonition to "obey without question" could be misunderstood or twisted for evil purposes.

Bonhoeffer thought the natural protection from such manipulation was to emphasize that obedience to Christ includes living within Christian community, where others can help us grow in Christ and anchor us to the biblical interpretation of obedience. Jesus intends for us to operate within the Body of Christ, holding each other accountable for our decisions (as "iron sharpens iron," Proverbs 27:17). About a year after *Discipleship*, Bonhoeffer wrote *Life Together* in order to explain that living in fellowship with other believers is an essential ingredient to becoming Christ-like.

May this book be God's instrument to draw us into the authentic, transparent community that is necessary for us to grow toward maturity in Christ.

Jon Walker
Jacob's Landing
June 2011

CHAPTER 1

WE WERE CREATED TO LIVE IN VISIBLE CHRISTIAN COMMUNITY

We belong to [Jesus] because we are in him. That is why the Scriptures call us the Body of Christ. . . . We who live here in fellowship with him will one day be with him in eternal fellowship. He who looks upon his brother should know that he will be eternally united with him in Jesus Christ.

—DIETRICH BONHOEFFER

"So it is with Christ's body. We are many parts of one body, and we all belong to each other."

—ROMANS 12:5B (NLT)

The Big Idea: God created us to live together in community, so thoroughly and unconditionally interdependent on each other that we operate as if we are parts of a Body moving together for one purpose. If we are cut-off from the Body, it is no different than a leg or foot being severed from our own bodies. The amputated limb must be reconnected as quickly as possible or it will not survive.

—∿∿—

When you feel lonely, that's a message from God. We were never meant to live life alone. In truth, God designed us to need the help of other believers in order to mature into the fullness of Christ. There is no such thing as independent study in the curriculum of Christ. We are connected to Jesus and connected to each other the moment we agree to follow after Jesus.

God designed us with a deep desire for relationships in order to drive us into an intimate commitment with Christ but then also one another in the Body of Christ. This loneliness is not a weakness; rather, it is evidence of God at work within us, calling us home to him.

We do all kinds of things to put an end to our loneliness, often chasing after wrong relationships or accepting superficial friend- ships, but God will not allow us to be satisfied with anything less than a life together with other believers, living, to use Bonhoeffer's phrase, "in visible" community with one another.

We are created as a race of beings to love and to be loved. God said, *"Let us make human beings in our image, make them reflecting our nature . . ."* (Genesis 1:26 MSG) The Father, Son, and Holy Spirit show us the loving nature of true community: All have equal value, each looks out for the other, one is ever ready to sacrifice for the sake of someone else, and everyone is absolutely safe. It is fully free and uninhibited expression of godly love.

We are designed to be at home in God's perfect love and to be part of a loving community on earth, where there is intimacy, harmony, fellowship, and friendship. The only way such a genuine community is possible is because of God's love in us.

The apostle Paul says, *"We take our lead from Christ, who is the source of everything we do. He keeps us in step with each other. His very breath and blood flow through us, nourishing us so that we will grow up healthy in God, robust in love"* (Ephesians 4:15b–16 MSG).

Paul compares our community to a body: *"So since we find ourselves fashioned into all these excellently formed and marvelously functioning parts in Christ's body, let's just go ahead and be what we were made to be, without enviously or pridefully comparing ourselves with each other, or trying to be something we aren't"* (Romans 12: 5b-6 MSG).

It is a paradox of our faith that we find our unique and specific purpose in life only after we yield our individualism for the good of many. We become one heart and mind with God and with other believers, and in the safety of that community, our true value as individuals will emerge (John 17:21–22).

We encourage people to accept their individuality (to be themselves) and yet reject individualism (living for themselves). It is that acceptance—the way Christ accepted us—that encourages us toward spiritual maturity, and we grow into that maturity, not as individuals, but as vital, participatory members of the Body of Christ, where *"each of us finds our meaning and function as a part of his body"* (Romans 12:5a MSG).

This means every believer is an indispensable, interconnected member of the Body, each of us critically dependent on each other. We live in an age when dependence is often seen as weakness, but Jesus sees dependence as strength. He knows it leads to intimacy and trust. He knows we were created to need each other and to need him.

Jesus finds his strength, power, and meaning in his dependence on the Father. Does that reflect a weakness in Jesus or faithful obedience? We are dependent on air. Is that a weakness of character on our part?

And Jesus is *voluntarily* dependent on us. Just as *"Christ is the visible image of the invisible God,"* we become the visible image of Christ to the world. Now that Jesus has returned to heaven and is no longer *"visible in the world,"* we live in visible fellowship as Christ's Body (Colossians 1:15 NLT; John 17:11-12 MSG; Ephesians 5:8-14 NIV). And God says the world will know we are the Body of Christ by how we love one another as we live together.

It is important to know that nearly every use of the word *church* in the New Testament refers to a local, visible congregation. The apostle Paul says, *"As a chopped-off finger or cut-off toe we wouldn't amount to much, would we?"* (Romans 12:5b MSG). But that's where we find ourselves when we distance ourselves from other believers. Chopped-off fingers and cut-off toes don't last long on their own. To survive, they must be reconnected to the body as quickly as possible. We must be connected to a local church—to a body of believers—in order to survive spiritually.

Jesus is . . .

Jesus says, *"The Father and I are one"* (John 10:30 TEV). This means he is so thoroughly submitted to the will of God that, when you look at Jesus, it is like you are looking at the Father (John 14:9). But this is not a metaphorical connection. It is a real and actual connection between Jesus and the Father.

To be like Jesus . . .

Jesus tells the Father, *"I in them and you in me, so that they may be completely one, in order that the world may know that you sent me and that you love them as you love me"* (John 17:23 TEV). When we submit our lives to Jesus, we become one with him and one with the Father. This is not some New Age, mystical, "we become gods" mythology; rather, the same Holy Spirit at work in you is at work in me, and that connects us together as one in the Body of Christ.

Scripture:

"We take our lead from Christ, who is the source of everything we do. He keeps us in step with each other. His very breath and blood flow through us, nourishing us so that we will grow up healthy in God, robust in love." Ephesians 4:15b–16 MSG

Questions:

If you slipped and sliced open your leg, what would you say to it? "I hope you feel better." "Hey, leg, I'll try to help you next week." How does this analogy change your thinking on Christian community?

CHAPTER 2

WE WERE CREATED TO SHARE GOD'S GRACE TOGETHER

It is by the grace of God that a congregation is permitted to gather visibly in this world to share God's Word and sacrament.
—DIETRICH BONHOEFFER

"But if we walk in the light, God himself being the light, we also experience a shared life with one another, as the sacrificed blood of Jesus, God's Son, purges all our sin."
—1 JOHN 1:7 (MSG)

The Big Idea: God's love in us makes genuine community possible. Like our salvation, this community is a gift from God. We cannot create it on our own, and that means we have to get past the idea that we create the community by merely getting together. We are in visible fellowship with each other because Jesus connects us to each other—period.

It is humanly impossible to break through to an authentic, transparent Life Together without the presence of Jesus. Unless he is at the center of our community, we are nothing more than a cookie and coffee society. Even if we work together on a great cause, that does not mean we're a God-centered, God-driven, grace-filled community that offers the uncommon safety and acceptance of Jesus.

While in this world, our Christian community is meant to reflect heaven, a place where we will celebrate God, who is Perfect Life and Perfect Love, a place where each and every believer will be fully matured in Christ. And so our Christ-community here on earth is meant to celebrate the life of Christ we share in common.

In visible fellowship, we help each other mature into Christians who are full of the grace and truth of Jesus (Colossians 1:28-29; Galatians 2:20-21). In visible fellowship, God makes use of all things—pain and suffering, joy and comfort, opposition and cooperation—to reproduce and express the life of Christ in us.

We also learn to allow the love of Christ to have the final say in all our relationships and in all the things we do. We learn to love as Christ loves. All of this prepares us to reign with him, by the rule of love, throughout all eternity.

Through Jesus, God enters into a personal union with each one of us and that creates the community that we share together. Our fellowship is a gift of God's grace. Bonhoeffer notes, "Not all Christians receive this blessing. The imprisoned, the sick, the scattered lonely, the proclaimers of the Gospel in heathen lands stand alone. They know that visible fellowship is a blessing."

In the Psalms, King David laments the times he is not in community: *"My heart breaks when I remember the past, when I went with the crowds to the house of God and led them as they walked along, a happy crowd, singing and shouting praise to God"* (Psalms 42:4 TEV). The apostle Paul suggests it is in those very moments that our prayers, letters, and blessings to believers who are separated from the visible community are critically important—so they will know they are still valued members in the Body of Christ.

Bonhoeffer notes that the apostle John, even in the loneliness of the island prison Patmos, was still able to celebrate our Life Together as believers by joining, in the Spirit, the heavenly worship of his congregations. Bonhoeffer says, "He sees the seven candlesticks, his congregations, the seven stars, the angels of the congregations, and in the midst and above it all the Son of Man, Jesus Christ, in all the splendor of the resurrection. He strengthens and fortifies him by His Word. This is the heavenly fellowship, shared by the exile on the day of his Lord's resurrection."

And God will sometimes scatter the community in order to plant new seeds of fellowship, such as when the early Christians were driven from Rome: *"Though I have scattered them among the nations, yet in far-off places they will remember me. They and their children will survive and return home together"* (Zechariah 10:8-9 TEV).

Clearly, God does not want us isolated in a Christian ghetto. Our love for one another is a witness to the world. The world will know we belong to God because of our love for one another.

For example, in Acts, we see believers in visible fellowship attracting the attention of non-believers: *"And all the believers lived in a wonderful harmony, holding everything in common. They sold whatever they owned and pooled their resources so that each person's need was met. They followed a daily discipline of worship in the Temple followed by meals at home, every meal a celebration, exuberant and joyful, as they praised God. People in general liked what they saw. Every day their number grew as God added those who were saved"* (Acts 2:44-47 MSG).

Jesus is . . .

Jesus maintains an intimate, obedient relationship with the Father, and he wants us to develop an intimate, obedient relationship with him. Our relationship with Jesus, then, allows us to develop an intimate, transparent relationship with one another. Our fellowship with other believers is God's gift, given to help us grow fully-matured into the image of Christ.

To be like Jesus . . .

We must be unconditionally committed to one another, to a local Body of Christ, in order to grow in Christ-like character. We must develop a grateful heart for God's gift to us of one another.

Scripture:

"But if we walk in the light, God himself being the light, we also experience a shared life with one another, as the sacrificed blood of Jesus, God's Son, purges all our sin." 1 John 1:7 MSG

Questions:

How will your relationship with other believers change now that you know they are God's gift to you? How does that change your relationship to believers who seem unlovable? If community is created by the presence of Christ, not by social connections or affinity groups, how does that change the way you interact in your small group?

CHAPTER 3

WE WERE CREATED FOR THE LIFE OF JESUS TO LIVE INSIDE US

Christianity means community through Jesus Christ and in Jesus Christ. No Christian community is more or less than this. Whether it be a brief, single encounter or the daily fellowship of years, Christian community is only this. We belong to one another only through and in Jesus Christ.

—DIETRICH BONHOEFFER

"Live in me. Make your home in me just as I do in you. In the same way that a branch can't bear grapes by itself but only by being joined to the vine, you can't bear fruit unless you are joined with me."

—JOHN 15:4 (MSG)

The Big Idea: The Life of the Father flows through Jesus into you, and it flows from the Father through Jesus into every other believer. This connects us in a real, authentic community that is based solely and wholly on our relationship to Jesus. Without our connection to the Vine, we can do nothing. When we are connected to the Vine, we can do all things.

—∿∿—

As a believer, you are now connected to the Divine nature through the work of Jesus Christ (John 10:10; John 4:14). Paul describes this as *"Christ in you, the hope of glory"* (Colossians 1:27 NIV). But it also means we are *"in Christ,"* becoming one with Jesus in the Spirit. This doesn't mean a *Kumbaya* kind of don't-we-all-feel-good-together oneness; it is an actual union with Christ that guides us to line up with the Word of God (1 Corinthians 6:17).

Jesus says, *"I in them and you in me—so that they may be brought to complete unity. Then the world will know that you sent me and have loved them even as you have loved me."* (John 17:23 NIV). Christ crucified is now Christ risen, and Christ risen sends the Holy Spirit to you, uniting you with him and uniting you with other believers, like a vine unites its branches together (John 16:7; John 15:1-8).

Jesus says the Father is the farmer, explaining, *"I am the Vine, you are the branches. When you're joined with me and I with you, the relation intimate and organic, the harvest is sure to be abundant. Separated, you can't produce a thing"* (John 15:5 MSG). It is only because we are *"in Christ"* that we can be a fruitful, authentic, genuine community. As we've discussed, when we are disconnected from the Vine, we are nothing more than a cookie and coffee social.

In community with Christ, the Holy Spirit enables us to live together *in visible* fellowship. The Spirit runs from the Vine to the branches, energizing us to live as God intended us to live. The Spirit teaches us how to align with God's agenda—and then prompts us to stay in alignment with Jesus and the Father.

Because we carry Jesus inside us, we are to strengthen each other and to challenge each other to do the greater things God created us to do. We're able to do the good work of serving one another on behalf of Jesus. As an example, our interdependence means on the days that I struggle with my trust in God, you, full of the grace and truth of Jesus, will be able to encourage me into greater faithfulness. On the days you struggle with your trust in God, I can help you back to a place of deeper belief.

Being *"in Christ"* enables you to see others in the Body of Christ as eternal beings designed by God for a purpose—no different from yourself. We no longer *"evaluate people by what they have or how they look. We looked at the Messiah that way once and got it all wrong, as you know. We certainly don't look at him that way anymore. Now we look inside, and what we see is that anyone united with the Messiah gets a fresh start, is created new. The old life is gone; a new life burgeons!"* (2 Corinthians 5:16-17 MSG).

This means the person you have difficulty getting along with in your small group, your congregation, even your family is, essentially, the voice of Jesus calling you to become more like him. Jesus is pushing you to look past the faults and sin of the other person and to look into the reality that this person who seems like chalk-screeching-on-a-blackboard to you is someone Jesus died to save. In truth, even while you were like chalk-screeching-on-a-blackboard, Christ died for you.

Bonhoeffer says, "The more genuine and the deeper our community becomes, the more will everything else between us recede, the more clearly and purely will Jesus Christ and his work become the one and only thing that is vital between us."

And it is essential to understand that our community in Christ is a spiritual community, not a social one. We are drawn together and connected by our belief in Jesus, not by the interest or hobbies we have in common.

Jesus is . . .

Jesus is the mediator between God and us, and between us and the other "branches." Jesus says, *"Live in me. Make your home in me just as I do in you. In the same way that a branch can't bear grapes by itself but only by being joined to the vine, you can't bear fruit unless you are joined with me"* (John 15:4 MSG).

To be like Jesus . . .

We are directly connected to the Life of Christ, which is placed within us when we submit our lives to him. His Life working in us enables us to live in visible fellowship with each other.

Scripture:

"But if you make yourselves at home with me and my words are at home in you, you can be sure that whatever you ask will be listened to and acted upon. This is how my Father shows who he is—when you produce grapes, when you mature as my disciples." John 15:7-8 MSG

Questions:

Jesus says we are wholly and totally dependent upon him to develop real, true, authentic, transparent relationships with each other. How does this change the way you look at relationships? How will this change the relationships you have with other believers? How might this change the dynamics of your small group? Why might you be fearful of authentic, transparent relationships?

CHAPTER 4

WE WERE CREATED TO LIVE IN THE REALITY OF CHRISTIAN COMMUNITY

Christian brotherhood is not an ideal that we must realize; it is rather a reality created by God in Christ in which we may participate. The more clearly we learn to recognize that the ground and strength and promise of all our fellowship is in Jesus Christ alone, the more serenely shall we think of our fellowship and pray and hope for it.

—DIETRICH BONHOEFFER

"God is light, and there is no darkness at all in him. If, then, we say that we have fellowship with him, yet at the same time live in the darkness, we are lying both in our words and in our actions. But if we live in the light—just as he is in the light—then we have fellowship with one another, and the blood of Jesus, his Son, purifies us from every sin."

—1 JOHN 1:5-7 (TEV)

The Big Idea: We must abandon our own opinion of what Christian community should be and live in the divine reality of what God created it to be. If we insist the community must match our ideal or fantasy, we will keep our fellowship from becoming authentic, transparent, and Christ-centered.

—∿—

Some of us enter Christian fellowship with a fantasy of what it should be like. We imagine everyone will be spiritually mature, everyone will get along with each other, everyone will be sensitive to the needs of others, and we'll all love and support each other.

But that's just an ideal we hold in our heads and has nothing to do with the divine reality of Christian community. So God sets about destroying the myth so that we can get into the reality of his design.

We cannot create Christian community in our own image, fashioning it into something that feels right to us. Bonhoeffer says, "One who wants more than what Christ has established does not want Christian brotherhood. He is looking for some extraordinary social experience which he has not found elsewhere; he is bringing muddled and impure desires into Christian brotherhood."

He notes our intentions can never be better than God's reality, and so "God's grace speedily shatters such dreams. Just as surely as God desires to lead us to a knowledge of genuine Christian fellowship, so surely must we be overwhelmed by a great disillusionment with others, with Christians in general, and, if we are fortunate, with ourselves."

The point at which we reach this disillusionment is the point at which we can finally get to the reality of Christ community. We come to Christ broken, knowing we are in desperate need of a savior, and we must enter Christian fellowship in that same brokenness, understanding that we only enter Christ community through our relationship with Jesus.

But this is also joyful news because the visible evidence that we have entered the Body of Christ is the authentic and transparent fellowship we have together. We now know the divine reality, that we are beloved children of God fashioned to take our place in the Body of Christ and to contribute in a unique way.

The sooner we get to this reality, the better off we are both individually and as a community because, Bonhoeffer notes, "He who loves his dream of a community more than the Christian community itself becomes a destroyer of the latter, even though his personal intentions may be ever so honest and earnest and sacrificial."

Our fantasies will eat away at the authenticity and transparency required in any Christ-centered fellowship. There is no way others can meet our ideal and so we become frustrated that no one is *acting* like a Christian ought to act.

Bonhoeffer notes that our discouragement leads to accusing others, and eventually accusing God, about the sorry state of our Christian community. This, then, lead to devilish despair, where we begin to accuse ourselves because we cannot match the ideal and we come to doubt if Christian community is even possible. The truth is it is impossible unless it is created from God's vision.

When the walls of our fantasy come tumbling down, Bonhoeffer says we can rejoice that none of us "can ever live by our own words and deeds, but only by that one Word and Deed which really binds us together—the forgiveness of sins in Jesus Christ. . . . When the morning mists of dreams vanish, then dawns the bright day of Christian fellowship."

We are finally able to enter our fellowship, "not as demanders but as thankful recipients." We can receive the "daily bread" of Christian fellowship with gratitude rather than attitude, and Bonhoeffer says this will prove we are ready to be trusted with the greater things God has planned for us. Indeed, our fellowship together is meant to be a reflection of our eternal fellowship in heaven, and Jesus is preparing us for that.

Bonhoeffer says complaints and ingratitude only "hinder God from letting our fellowship grow according to the measure and riches which are there for us all in Jesus Christ." Instead, we must learn to see the things that God sees. "What may appear weak and trifling to us may be great and glorious to God," says Bonhoeffer.

The critical point is that our community *in Christ* is a spiritual reality, not a human reality. In other words, it's not based on human nature, but on Jesus being present in our hearts: *"If we live in the light—just as he is in the light—then we have fellowship with one another, and the blood of Jesus, his Son, purifies us from every sin"* (1 John 1:7 TEV).

Our fellowship only works when we obediently trust Jesus to lead us into the uncommon safety of God's love, and safe within God's love:

- We can learn to love one another so deeply and so richly that we prove to the world we are truly connected to Christ.
- We can love the seemingly unlovable members of our Christ-community in the same way that Jesus loved us even when we were unlovable.
- We can attempt things that are impossible unless God gives us his strength to do them.

- We can change our priorities to match God's priorities, sacrificing, in faith, what we cannot keep for the things that can never be taken away.

Jesus is . . .

We only enter Christian fellowship through Jesus, and Jesus establishes our fellowship according to God's design. Jesus creates our fellowship as a spiritual reality.

To be like Jesus . . .

Our fellowship together is visible evidence we have entered the Body of Christ. It is a witness to how the Body works together in submission to Christ. In order to become like Christ, we must abandon our fantasies of a fellowship based on human nature and accept that we have entered a spiritual reality full of grace.

Scripture:

"God is light, and there is no darkness at all in him. If, then, we say that we have fellowship with him, yet at the same time live in the darkness, we are lying both in our words and in our actions. But if we live in the light—just as he is in the light—then we have fellowship with one another, and the blood of Jesus, his Son, purifies us from every sin." 1 John 1:5-7 TEV

Questions:

If someone insisting on her or his ideal of Christian fellowship becomes disillusioned and leaves the church, what would you say in an attempt to bring him or her back into the community? What frustrates you about Christian fellowship? Is it possible your frustrations stem from a bit of fantasy still in your head? What do you think it means that our fellowship is a spiritual reality?

CHAPTER 5

We Were Created to Learn How to Love in Christ-community

Because spiritual love does not desire but rather serves, it loves an enemy as a brother. It originates neither in the brother nor in the enemy but in Christ and his Word. Human love can never understand spiritual love, for spiritual love is from above; it is something completely strange, new, and incomprehensible to all earthly love.

—Dietrich Bonhoeffer

"The command we have from Christ is blunt: Loving God includes loving people. You've got to love both."

—1 John 4:13-21 (MSG)

The Big Idea: With Jesus, love always sets the agenda. He is God-centered and other-focused. On the other hand, we tend to let self-interest set the agenda, even if we call it love. God puts us in community so that we will learn to love one another through an unconditional commitment to each other.

—∿∿—

Consider a young girl with a crush. She says she loves him, but what she means is she wants to capture him by any means. She wants to be irresistible to him, to rule him with her love. She will do anything, not for him, but to get him. And when her love is not reciprocated, it will quickly turn to hate and jealousy.

But this adolescent love is not far removed from the love we often offer in our congregations and our small groups. It is a love that wants to re-create others into the image of what we think they should be.

And this kind of love, says Bonhoeffer, "makes itself an end in itself. It nurses and cultivates an ideal, it loves itself, and nothing else in the world." But "spiritual love proves itself in that everything it says and does commends Christ. It will not seek to move others by all too personal, direct influence, by impure interference in the life of another."

When we love others with spiritual love, Bonhoeffer notes we will "meet the other person with the clear Word of God and be ready to leave him alone with this Word for a long time, willing to release him again in order that Christ may deal with him."

On the other hand, Bonhoeffer says, "Human love has little regard for truth. It makes the truth relative, since nothing, not even the truth, must come between it and the beloved person. Human love desires and demands." He adds that human love is incapable of loving an enemy; in fact, it will make an enemy of those who resist it (consider the young adolescent scorned).

Spiritual love flows from Jesus Christ and it serves him alone. And, therefore, Bonhoeffer says, only Jesus can tell us what love is: "Where Christ bids me to maintain fellowship for the sake of love, I will maintain it. Where his truth enjoins me to dissolve a fellowship for love's sake, there I will dissolve it, despite all the protests of my human love."

In order for authentic, biblical community to develop, we must be reconditioned by the Spirit to love others like Jesus loves us. "Spiritual love recognizes the true image of the other person which he has received from Jesus Christ," says Bonhoeffer. The apostle John teaches, if we know God, then we will love others with the love of God (1 John 4:7).

Such unconditional love requires faith because it is beyond our own capabilities. It is an all-inclusive love. In fact, Bonhoeffer says, "The exclusion of the weak and insignificant, the seemingly useless people, from a Christian community may actually mean the exclusion of Christ; in the poor brother Christ is knocking at the door."

It is fear that keeps us from loving the weak and insignificant, but the apostle John says, *"There is no room in love for fear. Well-formed love banishes fear. Since fear is crippling, a fearful life—fear of death, fear of judgment—is one not yet fully formed in love. We, though, are going to love—love and be loved. First we were loved, now we love. He loved us first"* (1 John 4:18-19 MSG).

He adds that if we won't love someone we can see, then it is unlikely we love the God we can't see (1 John 4:19-21 MSG). "The command we have from Christ is blunt," says John. "Loving God includes loving people. You've got to love both" (1 John 4:21 MSG).

In addition, Bonhoeffer says our love for one another must be day-to-day. We will all have mountaintop experiences, but these are a "gracious extra beyond the daily bread of Christian community life." We should not live together for these experiences or even set the goal of experiencing them. "We are bound together by faith, not by experience," Bonhoeffer says.

And this is just the way God planned it, that the day-to-day fits into the larger spiritual reality of our fellowship; the spiritual reality is and was never meant to be secondary add-on to the day-to-day. Our community is a spiritual community and nothing else.

As a result, it is God himself who teaches us how to love one another: *"There is no need to write you about love for each other. You yourselves have been taught by God how you should love one another"* (1 Thessalonians 4:9 TEV).

The apostle Paul explains it this way: *"So here's what I want you to do, God helping you: Take your everyday, ordinary life—your sleeping, eating, going-to-work, and walking-around life—and place it before God as an offering. Embracing what God does for you is the best thing you can do for him"* (Romans 12:1 MSG).

Jesus is . . .

The love of God that is in Christ Jesus is the love we can never be separated from, not even by *"death or life, angels or rulers, things present or things to come, [hostile] powers, height or depth, or any other created thing. . ."* (Romans 8:38-39 HCSB). Jesus shows us that the only thing that *"matters is faith working through love"* (Galatians 5:6 HCSB).

To be like Jesus . . .

God himself teaches us how to love one another: *"There is no need to write you about love for each other. You yourselves have been taught by God how you should love one another"* (1 Thessalonians 4:9 TEV).

Scripture:

"The command we have from Christ is blunt: Loving God includes loving people. You've got to love both." (1 John 4:21 MSG)

Questions:

God himself teaches you to love others. What has God been teaching you lately about love? The Bible says, "When we take up permanent residence in a life of love, we live in God and God lives in us" (1 John 4:17 MSG). What do you think it means to take up permanent residence in a life of love? How does your view of your small group change now that you know it is part of a spiritual reality, not based on human nature?

CHAPTER 6

THE DAY'S BEGINNING: MORNING PRAISE

The Old Testament day begins at evening and ends with the going down of the sun. It is the time of expectation. The day of the New Testament church begins with the break of day and ends with the dawning light of the next morning. It is the time of fulfillment, the resurrection of the Lord. At night Christ was born, a light in darkness; noonday turned to night when Christ suffered and died on the Cross. But in the dawn of Easter morning Christ rose in victory from the grave.

—DIETRICH BONHOEFFER

"Because of the Lord's great love we are not consumed, for his compassions never fail. They are new every morning; great is your faithfulness."

—LAMENTATIONS 3:22–23 (NIV)

The Big Idea: Bonhoeffer says our day should begin with morning praise, a time with God's Word, praise for the Father, and communal prayer. God's mercies are fresh each morning, so our relationship with him is renewed each day.

(Note: The next few chapters may present ideas that seem quaint or archaic to our modern sensibilities, but the major point to remember is that these are methods to help us focus on God throughout the day. So often we live as if the spiritual is an add-on to our day when, in truth, the spiritual is our day and everything we do should reflect this. In addition, the idea of an extensive morning worship may seem impractical in our modern setting, but rather than dismiss the entire idea, we have to wonder why it is so difficult for most of us to spend more than a few minutes with God at the beginning of the day.)

Imagine you are in a situation where you aren't certain you will make it safely through the night. As the shadows set in, you know your chances of survival will diminish with the darkness. You cling to hope and you wait. *"Before sunrise I call to you for help; I place my hope in your promise"* (Psalm 119:147 TEV).

And then you see the darkness is getting less dark, as if the light is coming. You look to the horizon and you see a sliver of sunlight chasing the darkness away. You've made it to the morning. You will survive. It is a new day.

How would you celebrate this day beginning? Bonhoeffer argues that the joy and gratitude we would have in such a moment is the way we should start every day of our life in Christ. You celebrate, knowing God's *"saving power will rise on you like the sun and bring healing like the sun's rays. You will be as free and happy as calves let out of a stall"* (Malachi 4:2 TEV).

Bonhoeffer says, "If we were to learn again something of the praise and adoration that is due the triune God at break of day, God the Father and Creator, who has preserved our life through the dark night and wakened us to a new day, God the Son and

Savior, who conquered death and hell for us and dwells in our midst as Victor, God the Holy Spirit, who pours the bright gleam of God's Word into our hearts at the dawn of day, driving away all darkness and sin and teaching us to pray aright . . . then we would also begin to sense something of the joy that comes when night is past and brethren who dwell together in unity come together early in the morning for common praise of their God, common hearing of the Word, and common prayer."

The morning, then, does not belong to the individual. It is not ours to use as our own, as if we have a right to a cup of coffee, the morning news shows, or whatever else we do to start the day. Morning belongs to God and morning belongs to our Christ-community, even if at daybreak it is represented by our families.

God created the morning so we could enter into a common, communal praise (just as if we'd survived an uncertain night). Our life in Christ should be the central focus of our day—starting from the moment we awake.

"Therefore, at the beginning of the day let all distraction and empty talk be silenced and let the first thought and the first word belong to him to whom our whole life belongs," says Bonhoeffer. Like the poet-king David, we sing praises to the Father: *"I have complete confidence, O God; I will sing and praise you! Wake up, my soul! Wake up, my harp and lyre! I will wake up the sun"* (Psalm 57:7-8 TEV).

Think about this: Can you imagine Jesus being too busy to pray in the morning, gulping down a cup of coffee and thinking, "I've got so much to do today. When is there time to talk to the Father?" If we are learning to be like Christ, then we have to learn that our intimacy with the Father always takes priority. God says it is foolish to succumb to the tyranny of the urgent in the morning:

"It is useless to work so hard for a living, getting up early and going to bed late. For the LORD provides for those he loves, while they are asleep" (Psalm 127:2 TEV).

Spending time with God in the morning should be a normal part of life, Bonhoeffer says: "With remarkable frequency the Scriptures remind us that the men of God rose early to seek God and carry out His commands, as did Abraham, Jacob, Moses, and Joshua (cf. Genesis 19:27, 22:3; Exodus 8:16, 9:13, 24:4; Joshua 3:1, 6:12)." And the Bible tells us that Jesus made it a daily habit: *"Very early the next morning, long before daylight, Jesus got up and left the house. He went out of town to a lonely place, where he prayed"* (Mark 1:35 TEV).

Jesus is . . .

Jesus desired intimacy with God. His attitude is reflected in Psalm 63: *"O God, you are my God, and I long for you. My whole being desires you; like a dry, worn-out, and waterless land, my soul is thirsty for you"* (Psalm 63:1 TEV).

To be like Jesus . . .

"Christ's message in all its richness must live in your hearts. Teach and instruct one another with all wisdom. Sing psalms, hymns, and sacred songs; sing to God with thanksgiving in your hearts. Everything you do or say, then, should be done in the name of the Lord Jesus, as you give thanks through him to God the Father" (Colossians 3:16-17 TEV).

Scripture:

"Before sunrise I call to you for help; I place my hope in your promise." (Psalm 119:147 TEV)

Questions:

No doubt you already see the need to spend time with God in the morning. What are the things that keep you from being consistent in morning devotions? How could you work within your small group to help each other become consistent at morning devotionals? What about within your family?

CHAPTER 7

THE DAY'S BEGINNING: PRAYING THE PSALMS

This insight the New Testament and the Church have always recognized and declared. The Man Jesus Christ, to whom no affliction, no ill, no suffering is alien and who yet was the wholly innocent and righteous one, is praying in the Psalter through the mouth of his Church. The Psalter is the prayer book of Jesus Christ in the truest sense of the word. He prayed the Psalter and now it has become his prayer for all time.

—DIETRICH BONHOEFFER

"Speak to one another with the words of psalms, hymns, and sacred songs; sing hymns and psalms to the Lord with praise in your hearts."

—EPHESIANS 5:19-20 (TEV)

The Big Idea: Bonhoeffer says our day should begin with morning worship, a time with God's Word, singing praise to Jesus, and communal prayer. He says the Psalms are the great school of prayer because they are "the vicarious prayer of Christ for his Church," and so they should be part of a communal reading of God's Word.

—〰—

Bonhoeffer says, "By praying the Psalms, we can continue the prayers of Jesus here on earth." We join the prayers of Jesus, who is our intercessor before the Father. Bonhoeffer notes that the Psalms are the great school of prayer, teaching us how to pray beyond our experience, wisdom, or understanding. God says, *"I will instruct you and teach you in the way you should go; and I will counsel you with my loving eye on you"* (Psalm 32:8 NIV).

By praying the Psalms, we learn what it means to pray "in Christ." For instance, Bonhoeffer wonders who are we to pray the imprecatory psalms—with our sinful pasts and evil desires, plus the possibility even now of mixed motives? But, he adds, since Jesus took the vengeance of God upon himself and forgave his enemies and because Christ is in us, we can pray these prayers from the heart of Jesus.

Bonhoeffer says, "And how shall we pray those psalms of unspeakable misery and suffering, the meaning of which we have hardly begun to sense even remotely?"

He adds, "We can and we should pray the psalms of suffering, the psalms of the passion, not in order to generate in ourselves what our hearts do not know of their own experience, not to make our own laments, but because all this suffering was real and actual in Jesus Christ, because the Man Jesus Christ suffered sickness, pain, shame, and death, because in his suffering and death all flesh suffered and died."

The Psalms also teach us to pray as a fellowship. Some of us have experienced this through responsive reading during a worship service, where a leader reads specific verses and then the congregation responds by reading another set of verses.

The Bible teaches us to *"speak to one another with the words of psalms, hymns, and sacred songs; sing hymns and psalms to the Lord with praise in your hearts"* (Ephesians 5:19-20 TEV). Responsive reading is a reminder that we are never alone.

In addition, Bonhoeffer says the whole of Christ can be seen in the Psalms, "a whole which the individual can never fully comprehend and call his own." We read the Psalms because *"Christ's message in all its richness must live in [our] hearts"* (Colossians 3:16a TEV).

The Psalms teach us that *"the word of the Lord is right and true; he is faithful in all he does. The Lord loves righteousness and justice; the earth is full of his unfailing love"* (Psalm 33:4-5 NIV). They teach us that God is just, that he's pure and honest, that he never fails to fulfill a promise, and that he is trustworthy in everything he does.

Jesus is . . .

The Psalms collectively present a whole picture of Christ.

To be like Jesus . . .

By reading the Psalms, we get an intimate view of Jesus.

Scripture:

"Christ's message in all its richness must live in your hearts. Teach and instruct one another with all wisdom. Sing psalms, hymns, and sacred songs; sing to God with thanksgiving in your hearts." (Colossians 3:16 TEV)

Questions:

Why do you think the Psalms are a good school of prayer? How do you respond to the idea that the Psalms represent Christ's prayer for the church? What has been your experience with responsive reading? What is your favorite psalm? Why?

CHAPTER 8

THE DAY'S BEGINNING: GOD'S WORD

[Holy Scripture] is God's revealed Word for all men, for all times. Holy Scripture does not consist of individual passages; it is a unit and is intended to be used as such.

—DIETRICH BONHOEFFER

"All Scripture is inspired by God and is useful for teaching the truth, rebuking error, correcting faults, and giving instruction for right living, so that the person who serves God may be fully qualified and equipped to do every kind of good deed."

—2 TIMOTHY 3:16-17 (TEV)

The Big Idea: Bonhoeffer says our day should begin with morning worship, a time with God's Word, singing praise to Jesus, and communal prayer. Our common devotions should include a daily reading from the Psalms, the Old Testament, and the New Testament.

Bonhoeffer says there may be initial resistance to communal Bible reading, but it is important we develop the practice of getting into the Word, individually and collectively. Although some may argue this gives us too much Scripture to process daily, Bonhoeffer says that is a specious argument because every sentence, phrase, or word in Scripture is so full of multiple relationships with the whole of Scripture that every passage "far surpasses our understanding."

In addition, when we are engaged with the Word of God, we are engaged with Jesus. Bonhoeffer says, "As a whole the Scriptures are God's revealing Word. Only in the infiniteness of its inner relationships, in the connection of Old and New Testaments, of promise and fulfillment, sacrifice and law, law and gospel, cross and resurrection, faith and obedience, having and hoping, will the full witness to Jesus Christ the Lord be perceived."

In other words, the Bible is not mere "proverbial and practical wisdom," says Bonhoeffer. It is "God's revealing Word in Jesus Christ." The apostle Paul explains that Jesus is *"the key that opens all the hidden treasures of God's wisdom and knowledge"* (Colossians 2:3 TEV).

And because the Bible is a living corpus that expresses a portion of God's infinite mind, it is important we learn the whole context and connectedness of its inspired revelation. That way, Bonhoeffer says, we are pulled into "the wonderful world of revelation of the people of Israel with its prophets, judges, kings, and priests, its wars, festivals, sacrifices, and sufferings. The fellowship of believers is woven into the Christmas story, the baptism, the miracles and teaching, the suffering, dying, and rising again of Jesus Christ."

This means, Bonhoeffer says, "We are torn out of our own existence and set down in the midst of the holy history of God on earth. There God dealt with us, and there He still deals with us, our needs and our sins, in judgment and grace. It is not that God is the spectator and sharer of our present life, howsoever important that is; but rather that we are the reverent listeners and participants in God's action in the sacred story, the history of the Christ on earth."

Seeing what God has done through history and knowing what he has done for us develops our faith. In fact, Bonhoeffer says knowing what God did for Israel and what he did for us through Jesus Christ, his only begotten Son, is more important than seeking what God intends for us today.

The God-adventure is a sweeping dance of redemption showing how he moves through history coordinating circumstances and events in order to bring us home to him. God's story is a tear-filled romance where he chases after those he loves, regardless of whether they love him back. It's a nail-biting drama where he launches a rescue mission for his children, who are held in captivity, and he arrives in his perfectly planned nick of time.

In God's story, his children follow him in faith, yet even the most faithful stumble and fail. But the story doesn't end there! God redeems even the worst mistakes, making all things work together for the good of those he calls his own.

It is a story of majesty, power, and infinite grace; it's about a God who speaks the world into existence, sets the moon and the stars in place, yet who also cares for every detail of your life. Reading the Bible helps us to see and understand and live according to the scope and magnitude of God's grand adventure.

"The fact that Jesus Christ died is more important than the fact that I shall die, and the fact that Jesus Christ rose from the dead is the sole ground of my hope that I, too, shall be raised on the Last Day," says Bonhoeffer. "Our salvation is 'external to ourselves.' I find no salvation in my life history, but only in the history of Jesus Christ. Only he who allows himself to be found in Jesus Christ, in his incarnation, his Cross, and his resurrection, is with God and God with him."

We can only find certainty and confidence in Jesus and our salvation on biblical ground. "It is not our heart that determines our course, but God's Word," says Bonhoeffer. It is only with God's Word that we can help one another stay steadily on the narrow path following Jesus.

Because of God's Word we can be confident that our Father is just and loving and that he is actively at work in our lives. Because of God's Word we believe Jesus died and rose again, and that God will resurrect those in Christ (1 Thessalonians 4:13–18).

Bonhoeffer notes that we often hear people argue from experience or opinion when faced with a crucial decision; yet, even among believers the argument of Scripture is missing. If we give greater credence to experience or opinion, then we reveal we don't "seriously read, know, and study the Scriptures." Bonhoeffer says, "One who will not learn to handle the Bible for himself is not an evangelical Christian."

How should we read the Scriptures as a group? Bonhoeffer says:

- Various members can read in turn.
- Polished reading is not necessary; in fact, Bonhoeffer suggests a slow, stumbling reader far surpasses the highly polished reading by minister.
- We should approach the reading in humility. We shouldn't read as if we are the biblical writer speaking. This just makes us "rhetorical, emotional, sentimental,

or coercive and imperative." In other words, I will be directing the listeners' attention to myself instead of to the Word.

- Instead, we should read the Scriptures the way we would read a letter from a friend whom the fellowship knows. That way, even though one of us is reading it, we can all "hear" our friend's personality in the letter.

Bonhoeffer adds, "God's Word is to be heard by everyone in his own way and according to the measure of his understanding. A child hears and learns the Bible for the first time in family worship; the adult Christian learns it repeatedly and better, and he will never finish acquiring knowledge of its story."

Jesus is . . .

Jesus knew the Scriptures. He taught from them, mentioned them in conversation, used them in his arguments with religious leaders, and leaned on them when the devil tempted him.

To be like Jesus . . .

We must know the Scriptures. When we are engaged with the Word of God, we are engaged with Jesus.

Scripture:

"And you remember that ever since you were a child, you have known the Holy Scriptures, which are able to give you the wisdom that leads to salvation through faith in Christ Jesus. All Scripture is inspired by God and is useful for teaching the truth, rebuking error, correcting faults, and giving instruction for right living, so that the person who serves God may be fully qualified and equipped to do every kind of good deed." (2 Timothy 3:15-17 TEV)

Questions:

Bonhoeffer says, "One who will not learn to handle the Bible for himself is not an evangelical Christian." What do you think about this statement? Bonhoeffer says, "It is not our heart that determines our course, but God's Word." What do you think of this statement? If the Word of God is dynamic and living, what does that mean for your life?

CHAPTER 9

THE DAY'S BEGINNING: SINGING THE NEW SONG

God has prepared for Himself one great song of praise throughout eternity, and those who enter the community of God join in this song. It is the song that the *"morning stars sang together and all the sons of God shouted for joy"* at the creation of the world. (Job 38:7)

—DIETRICH BONHOEFFER

"Praise the LORD! Sing to the LORD a new song. Sing his praises in the assembly of the faithful."

—PSALM 149:1 (NLT)

The Big Idea: Bonhoeffer says our day should begin with morning worship, a time with God's Word, singing praise to Jesus, and communal prayer. He says we need to sing praises to God every morning, for this is how we join the heavenly choir: "This is singing from the heart, singing to the Lord, singing the Word; this is singing in unity."

Bonhoeffer says after we've prayed the psalms and read Scripture, we should sing hymns together. In this, we join the voice of the church, all the saints, both the great cloud of witnesses and those who are still on earth, praising, thanking, and praying to God in unity.

Just as God's mercies are renewed each morning, our song of praise is refreshed then also. Every day we have new reasons to praise and thank the Lord. "Praise the LORD! Sing to the LORD a new song. Sing his praises in the assembly of the faithful" (Psalm 149:1 NLT).

Bonhoeffer says our daily Christ-hymn "is the victory song of the children of Israel after passing through the Red Sea, the Magnificat of Mary after the annunciation, the song of Paul and Silas in the night of prison, the song of the singers on the sea of glass after their rescue, 'the song of Moses the servant of God, and the song of the Lamb'" (Revelation 15:3).

It is a song of heavenly fellowship, praising the triune God and the work of his hand. "On earth it is the song of those who believe, in heaven the song of those who see," Bonhoeffer says.

"Our new song is an earthly song, a song of pilgrims and wayfarers upon whom the Word of God has dawned to light their way," Bonhoeffer says. "Our earthly song is bound to God's revealing Word in Jesus Christ. It is the simple song of the children of this earth who have been called to be God's children; not ecstatic, not enraptured, but sober, grateful, reverent, addressed steadily to God's revealed Word."

The song should come from our hearts, overflowing with Christ. We "sing hymns and psalms to the Lord with praise in [our] hearts," surrendered to the Word and joined together in humility, discipline, and in Christian fellowship (Ephesians 5:19 TEV).

Bonhoeffer says, "Where the heart is not singing there is no melody, there is only the dreadful medley of human self-praise." He says our singing should remain simple. The focus is on Jesus and praising him with the words from our hearts. In other words, we don't need to make a production out of the songs we sing, where we end up drawing attention to the music.

At the same time, we should not become spectators to the singing. Bonhoeffer says, "Unison singing, difficult as it is, is less of a musical than a spiritual matter."

He says, "It is the voice of the Church that is heard in singing together. It is not you that sings, it is the Church that is singing, and you, as a member of the Church, may share in its song. Thus all singing together that is right must serve to widen our spiritual horizon, make us see our little company as a member of the great Christian Church on earth, and help us willingly and gladly to join our singing, be it feeble or good, to the song of the Church."

The apostle Paul gave an example of this communal praise, when he referred the Philippians to the song: *"Our attitude should be the same as Christ Jesus, who emptied himself of all the things that come with being a king, and instead made himself a lowly servant . . ."* (Paraphrase of Philippians 2:5-7).

Paul says there is "nothing between us and God, our faces shining with the brightness of his face. And so we are transfigured much like the Messiah, our lives gradually becoming brighter and more beautiful as God enters our lives and we become like him" (2 Corinthians 3:18 MSG).

Bonhoeffer says:

- We should alternate singing with Scripture readings and prayer.

- Unison singing will only work within our fellowship when everyone has an attitude of worship and discipline.
- Our singing should be in unison, that is, this is not a choir performance requiring complex parts. The point is to draw attention toward God, not to draw attention to our musical abilities.

Jesus is . . .

"They were standing by the sea of glass, holding harps that God had given them and singing the song of Moses, the servant of God, and the song of the Lamb: 'Lord God Almighty, how great and wonderful are your deeds! King of the nations, how right and true are your ways! Who will not stand in awe of you, Lord? Who will refuse to declare your greatness? You alone are holy. All the nations will come and worship you, because your just actions are seen by all'" (Revelation 15:2-4 TEV).

To be like Jesus . . .

Through Christian fellowship, we become a new song for Jesus: *"May our dependably steady and warmly personal God develop maturity in you so that you get along with each other as well as Jesus gets along with us all. Then we'll be a choir—not our voices only, but our very lives singing in harmony in a stunning anthem to the God and Father of our Master Jesus! So reach out and welcome one another to God's glory. Jesus did it; now you do it!"* (Romans 15:5-7 MSG).

Scripture:

"Praise the LORD! Sing to the LORD a new song. Sing his praises in the assembly of the faithful." Psalms 149:1 (NLT)

Questions:

Why is it important to know that unison singing is about unity? How can we find unity by singing together? What does it mean that our lives can become a new song for Jesus?

CHAPTER 10

THE DAY'S BEGINNING: SAYING OUR PRAYERS TOGETHER

We have heard God's Word, and we have been permitted to join in the hymn of the Church; but now we are to pray to God as a fellowship, and this prayer must really be our word, our prayer for this day, for our work, for our fellowship, for the particular needs and sins that oppress us in common, for the persons who are committed to our care.

—DIETRICH BONHOEFFER

"And I tell you more: whenever two of you on earth agree about anything you pray for, it will be done for you by my Father in heaven."

—MATTHEW 18:19 (TEV)

The Big Idea: Bonhoeffer says our day should begin with morning worship, a time with God's Word, singing praise to Jesus, and communal prayer. By praying together, we bring "the cares, the needs, the joys and thanksgivings, the petitions and hopes" of the whole group before God, supporting each other in collective intercession.

—⁓—

Since we live together under the Word of God, we should pray together as a family or fellowship. Our prayers should be devoid of ritual; instead, we should pray like a child talks to a parent. There is a familiarity there that means we don't have to think through how to say things, we can just share what is on our hearts. Our conversation should be free, conversational, and unpretentious.

Bonhoeffer suggests appointing one person at first to pray on behalf of the whole fellowship. He says this gets everyone past any "timidity about praying freely in one's own words in the presence of others. . . ." But he also says this doesn't mean we can't eventually pray as a group with many voices. And Bonhoeffer reminds us that God is just as pleased with a halting, stumbling prayer as he is with one that is articulate and smooth.

Either the head of the family, or someone designated for an extended period, can pray representing the group, but Bonhoeffer says there are conditions to this arrangement:

- The group must commit to interceding for the one who voices prayers on their behalf (implying these prayers may begin in private until others are comfortable praying in front of the group). Bonhoeffer asks, "How could one person pray the prayer of the fellowship without being steadied and upheld in prayer by the fellowship itself?"
- The group must agree that any word of criticism toward the one designated to pray on their behalf will be turned into intense intercession and sincere help.
- These communal prayers incorporate the needs of the whole group, so the one voicing prayer for the

community must be aware of the needs and concerns of others. This means the one who prays must be involved in the life of the fellowship, familiar with "the cares, the needs, the joys and thanksgivings, the petitions and hopes of the others."

- The one who prays should not be elevated above others in the group. He or she is simply praying on behalf of the group. This means the group must be active in helping and guiding the one who prays, offering "suggestions and requests to remember this or that need, or work, or even a particular person in the prayer." This will keep the one who prays from confusing his or her own heart with the heart of the fellowship.

- Communal prayer should have some semblance of order, such as following the outline of the Lord's Prayer, or praying from local needs to global concerns.

- The designated pray-er must commit to praying, no matter how he or she feels. "Otherwise, the prayer of the fellowship will too easily be governed by moods which have nothing to do with spiritual life," says Bonhoeffer.

- Bonhoeffer adds, "It is precisely when a person, who is borne down by inner emptiness and weariness or a sense of personal unworthiness, feels that he would like to withdraw from his task, that he should learn what it means to have a duty to perform in the fellowship, and the brethren should support him in his weakness, in his inability to pray."

- And the Bible says, *"In the same way the Spirit also comes to help us, weak as we are. For we do not know how we ought to pray; the Spirit himself pleads with God for us in groans that words cannot express"* (Romans 8:26 TEV). Jesus says the Father knows our needs even before we ask and that is an important point to remember when we approach God in prayer.

Bonhoeffer notes his concern that relying too heavily on ritual or prepared prayer will eventually become "an evasion of real prayer." In his book, *The Cost of Discipleship*, Bonhoeffer says, "It matters little what form of prayer we adopt or how many words we use, what matters is the faith which lays hold on God and touches the heart of the Father who knew us long before we came to him."

He adds, "Helpful as the Church's tradition of prayer is for learning to pray, it nevertheless cannot take the place of the prayer that I owe to God this day. Here the poorest mumbling utterance can be better than the best-formulated prayer.

Jesus is . . .

Jesus intercedes for us, and when we pray, we join Jesus in his prayers. He is the Mediator between God and us, and it is through Jesus that God hears our prayers.

To be like Jesus . . .

Because we join the prayers of Jesus, we can be certain that God will answer our prayers and fulfill his promises.

Scripture:

"In the same way the Spirit also comes to help us, weak as we are. For we do not know how we ought to pray; the Spirit himself pleads with God for us in groans that words cannot express." (Romans 8:26 TEV)

Questions:

Why do you think we should pray if God already knows our needs? What stops you or makes you hesitant to pray with others? How will your prayers change, knowing they should be free, conversational, and unpretentious?

CHAPTER 11

THE DAY'S BEGINNING: THE FELLOWSHIP OF THE TABLE

The table fellowship of Christians implies obligation. It is our daily bread that we eat, not my own. We share our bread. Thus we are firmly bound to one another not only in the Spirit but also in our whole physical being. The one bread that is given to our fellowship links us together in a firm covenant. Now none dares go hungry as long as another has bread, and he who breaks this fellowship of the physical life also breaks the fellowship of the Spirit.

—DIETRICH BONHOEFFER

"He sat down to eat with them, took the bread, and said the blessing; then he broke the bread and gave it to them. Then their eyes were opened and they recognized him, but he disappeared from their sight. They said to each other, 'Wasn't it like a fire burning in us when he talked to us on the road and explained the Scriptures to us?'"

—LUKE 24:30-32 (TEV)

The Big Idea: Bonhoeffer says our day should begin with morning worship, a time with God's Word, singing praise to Jesus, and communal prayer. In this way we are nourished and strengthened by the Bread of Life. Only then is it time for us to break our fast from food (breakfast). "Giving thanks and asking God's blessing, the Christian family receives its daily bread from the hand of the Lord."

Bonhoeffer says there are three reasons we gather for the fellowship of the table after our morning devotionals :

First, we're now fully focused on the truth that Jesus is the giver of all gifts. We've re-affirmed our trust that he is our Lord, the Son of God, and that he is the Bread of Life, who gives us our daily bread.

Second, this helps us understand that we received the gift of sustenance so that we can carry on the work of Jesus. This is why we are given the gift of our daily bread: It is so we will have the strength to do what God commands us to do and to fulfill the purpose for which God created us.

Third, we can confess the "gracious omnipresence of Jesus Christ," praying, "Come, Lord Jesus, be our guest." We can be grateful for the presence of God in our lives.

"So in a singular way, the daily table fellowship binds the Christians to their Lord and one another," Bonhoeffer says. Like the disciples who met Jesus on the road to Emmaus, we can know when we sit down at the table that it is Jesus who breaks the bread for us and, as a result, the eyes of our faith are opened.

Bonhoeffer says the fellowship of the table should have a festive quality. "It is a constantly recurring reminder in the midst of our everyday work of God's resting after His work, of the Sabbath as the meaning and goal of the week and its toil." Our lives are not just about work and duty; there is also "refreshment and joy in the goodness of God. We labor, but God nourishes and sustains us."

We're reminded that our provision comes from God and not from the work of our hands (Psalm 127:2). We're reminded that God wants to bless us, so we can eat our food with joy (Ecclesiastes 9:7).

"Through our daily meals He is calling us to rejoice, to keep holiday in the midst of our working day," Bonhoeffer says. God cannot endure that unfestive, mirthless attitude of ours in which we eat our bread in sorrow, with pretentious, busy haste, or even with shame.

Because God provides our daily bread, it is not our own and so we should willingly share what we have. Bonhoeffer says we are not only bound together in the spirit, but also physically. We are branches connected to the Jesus vine and his life flows through us, but there is also a physical connection between us. "The one bread that is given to our fellowship links us together in a firm covenant. Now none dares go hungry as long as another has bread, and he who breaks this fellowship of the physical life also breaks the fellowship of the Spirit."

The Bible says, *"Share your food with the hungry and open your homes to the homeless poor"* (Isaiah 58:7 TEV). Jesus says when we see those in our fellowship who are in need, we are seeing him: *"I tell you, whenever you did this for one of the least important of these followers of mine, you did it for me!"* (Matthew 25:40 TEV).

Bonhoeffer makes the observation that "not until one person desires to keep his own bread for himself does hunger ensue. This is a strange divine law." He adds, "The fellowship of the table teaches Christians that here they still eat the perishable bread of the earthly pilgrimage. But if they share this bread with one another, they shall also one day receive the imperishable bread together in the Father's house. 'Blessed is he that shall eat bread in the kingdom of God' (Luke 14:15)."

Jesus is . . .

Jesus is the Bread of Life who provides us with our daily bread.

To be like Jesus . . .

We must learn to be grateful each day, first, for the grace God gives us through Jesus, and then for the food God gives us daily.

Scripture:

"So go ahead. Eat your food with joy, and drink your wine with a happy heart, for God approves of this!" (Ecclesiastes 9:7 NLT)

Questions:

What do you think about the idea that the primary purpose for food is to sustain us to do the work of God? How will that change the way you eat? Respond to this statement: "Not until one person desires to keep his own bread for himself does hunger ensue."

CHAPTER 12

THE DAY'S WORK

Our strength and energy for work increase when we have prayed God to give us the strength we need for our daily work. . . . Decisions which our work demands will be simpler and easier when they are made, not in the fear of men, but solely in the presence of God.

—DIETRICH BONHOEFFER

"Whatever you do, work at it with all your heart, as though you were working for the Lord and not for people."
—COLOSSIANS 3:23 (TEV)

The Big Idea: God uses our work to strip away self-centeredness, forcing us to focus on tasks beyond ourselves. No matter what we do, our work becomes a form of worship when we work as if we are working for God.

———

When we work in our jobs as if we are working for God, every thing we do becomes a prayer. This is why Paul teaches us to pray without ceasing. We keep God present at all times, so that *"everything [we] do or say, then, should be done in the name of the*

Lord Jesus, as [we] give thanks through him to God the Father" (Colossians 3:17 TEV).

We seek his guidance on how to do what we do and how to express love to those with whom we work. Our prayers compel us *to "never be lazy, but work hard and serve the Lord enthusiastically"* (Romans 12:11 NLT).

Bonhoeffer says our unceasing prayers create a unity within the day, where we move from morning worship into our daily work. Unceasing prayer reminds us that the spiritual is not just an add-on to our day; rather, our day is a part of the greater spiritual reality. The apostle Paul teaches, *"So whether you eat or drink or whatever you do, do it all for the glory of God"* (1 Corinthians 10:31 NIV).

Rick Warren, author of *The Purpose Driven Life*, says, "It doesn't matter if you're rearranging papers or signing bills or changing a baby's diaper, any job can become an act of worship if you do it enthusiastically for God. No matter what you do, it's never just a job if you are a believer. This is because God designed you with talents, gifts and interests that He wants used for His glory."

Bonhoeffer says the time we spend in prayer in the morning determines the rest of our day:

- "The organization and distribution of our time will be better for having been rooted in prayer.
- The temptations which the working day brings with it will be overcome by this breakthrough to God.
- Even routine mechanical work will be performed more patiently when it is done with the knowledge of God and His command.
- Our strength and energy for work increase when we have prayed God to give us the strength we need for our daily work."

Jesus is . . .

Jesus saw his work as joining the work of God: *"My Father is still working, and I am working also"* (John 5:17b HCSB).

To be like Jesus . . .

"Work willingly at whatever you do, as though you were working for the Lord rather than for people. Remember that the Lord will give you an inheritance as your reward, and that the Master you are serving is Christ" (Colossians 3:23-24 NLT).

Scripture:

"May the favor of the Lord our God rest on us; establish the work of our hands for us—yes, establish the work of our hands." (Psalm 90:17 NIV)

Questions:

How would you interpret these verses:

- "May the favor of the Lord our God rest on us; establish the work of our hands for us—yes, establish the work of our hands" Psalm 90:17 (NIV).
- "Commit your actions to the Lord, and your plans will succeed" (Proverbs 16:3 NLT).
- "Meanwhile, men and women go out to work, busy at their jobs until evening. What a wildly wonderful world, GOD! You made it all, with Wisdom at your side, made earth overflow with your wonderful creations" Psalms 104:23-24 (MSG).

CHAPTER 13

MID-DAY WORSHIP

The noonday hour, where it is possible, becomes for the Christian family fellowship a brief rest on the day's march. Half of the day is past. The fellowship thanks God and prays for protection until the eventide. It receives its daily bread and prays, in the words of a Reformation hymn: Feed us, O Father, thy children, Comfort us, afflicted sinners.

—DIETRICH BONHOEFFER

"He sat down to eat with them, took the bread, and said the blessing; then he broke the bread and gave it to them. Then their eyes were opened and they recognized him, but he disappeared from their sight. They said to each other, 'Wasn't it like a fire burning in us when he talked to us on the road and explained the Scriptures to us?'"

—LUKE 24:30-32 (TEV)

The Big Idea: The day belongs to God, and so in the middle of the day we pause to thank God again for the many things he does for us and that he continues to provide us with our daily bread.

This is the day that the Lord has made and so the day belongs to him. He provides us with rest at noon and provides us with another meal. Bonhoeffer says this is "the token of the grace and faithfulness with which God supports and guides His children."

We cannot take it for granted that our work provides us with bread. Our daily bread comes through God's grace. He is not obligated to give us bread, although we are obligated to work (2 Thessalonians 3:10).

Bonhoeffer notes that the work of the atonement was nearing completion at noon (Matthew 27). In fact, significant things happen at noon in the New Testament.

- Jesus was resting at noonday by a well when the Samaritan woman came to fill her water jar (John 4).
- Pilate offered to release Jesus instead of Barabbas at noon (John 19).
- Peter was praying before the noon meal when the servants of Cornelius arrived, and Peter soon learned the gospel was for the Gentiles as well as the Jews (Acts 10).
- And Paul was blinded on the Damascus Road when Jesus spoke to him directly (Acts 22).

The point is, rather than stressing through our lunchtime (or midday break), we should thank Jesus for the meal he provides and the rest he allows. It is a time to re-center and re-energize and a time to enjoy fellowship with other believers. Jesus gives you permission to take a mid-day break, trusting that it will help you prioritize the rest of your day.

Jesus is . . .

Jesus gives us grace we do not deserve.

To be like Jesus . . .

We should rest in the grace of God and enjoy that rest with other believers.

Scripture:

"From noon to three, the whole earth was dark. Around mid-afternoon Jesus groaned out of the depths, crying loudly, "Eli, Eli, lama sabachthani?" which means, "My God, my God, why have you abandoned me?" (Matthew 27:45-46 MSG)

Questions:

What is your response to the truth that God provides your daily bread (and income), that it is not dependent on the work you do? How do you bring Jesus into your noonday meal? Have you ever thought of your lunchtime as rest provided by God?

CHAPTER 14

EVENING WORSHIP

It is the prayer that God may dwell with us and in us even though we are unconscious of His presence, that He may keep our hearts pure and holy in spite of all the cares and temptations of the night, to make our hearts ever alert to hear His call and, like the boy Samuel, answer Him even in the night: "Speak, Lord; for thy servant heareth" (I Sam. 3:9).

—DIETRICH BONHOEFFER

"The protector of Israel never dozes or sleeps. The LORD will guard you; he is by your side to protect you. The sun will not hurt you during the day, nor the moon during the night. The LORD will protect you from all danger; he will keep you safe. He will protect you as you come and go now and forever."

—PSALMS 121:4-8 (TEV)

The Big Idea: Bonhoeffer says we should end the day in the same way we started it: praying the Psalms, singing hymns, and sharing common prayer. The point, again, is that Jesus is not just an add-on to our day, where we give him a few minutes in the morning. Jesus isn't just part of our lives; he is our Life and so we should praise him first thing every morning and praise him before we go to bed at night.

⁓

We gather together again, and like the disciples on the road to Emmaus, we should tell Jesus each night, *"Stay with us; the day is almost over and it is getting dark.' So [Jesus] went in to stay with them"* (Luke 24:29 TEV). Bonhoeffer says Jesus should get the last word before we go to sleep, and so it is best for evening devotions to be right at the end of the day, a natural part of us getting ready for bed. "When night falls, the true light of God's Word shines brighter for the Church," adds Bonhoeffer.

Resting from the day's work, Bonhoeffer says "we pray God for the blessing, peace, and safety of all Christendom; for our congregation; for the pastor in his ministry; for the poor, the wretched, and lonely; for the sick and dying; for our neighbors, for our own folks at home, and for our fellowship."

In our weariness, we place ourselves into God's hand, trusting he continues to work while we sleep: *"The protector of Israel never dozes or sleeps"* (Psalm 121:4 TEV). Bonhoeffer says, "A day at a time is long enough to sustain one's faith; the next day will have its own cares."

We also take the time to be reconciled with one another, so that no one in our fellowship or family will carry their anger into the dark of night. The Bible tells us not to go to bed angry, so each evening should include a time for the asking and giving of forgiveness because, as Bonhoeffer notes, *"It is perilous for the Christian to lie down to sleep with an unreconciled heart"* (Ephesians 4:26).

Bonhoeffer notes that the ancient church profoundly prayed that, even when our eyes are closed in sleep, "God may nevertheless keep our hearts awake."

He says, "It is the prayer that God may dwell with us and in us even though we are unconscious of His presence, that He may keep our hearts pure and holy in spite of all the cares and temptations of the night, to make our hearts ever alert to hear His call and, like the boy Samuel, answer Him even in the night: 'Speak, LORD, your servant is listening'" (1 Samuel 3:9 TEV).

Jesus is . . .

Jesus is with us, dwelling in us, even when we are unconscious of his presence.

To be like Jesus . . .

Let us learn to trust that God is always at work, even when we are at rest.

Scripture:

"The protector of Israel never dozes or sleeps. The LORD will guard you; he is by your side to protect you. The sun will not hurt you during the day, nor the moon during the night. The LORD will protect you from all danger; he will keep you safe. He will protect you as you come and go now and forever." (Psalms 121:4-8 TEV)

Questions:

Bonhoeffer says, "In all the ancient evening prayers we are struck by the frequency with which we encounter the prayer for preservation during the night from the devil, from terror, and from an evil, sudden death. The ancients had a persistent sense of man's helplessness while sleeping, of the kinship of sleep with death, of the devil's cunning in making a man fall when he is defenseless." Why do you think we have lost this sense of protection from God?

Bonhoeffer says, "It is perilous for the Christian to lie down to sleep with an unreconciled heart." Why is that important?

CHAPTER 15

THE DAY ALONE: WHEN LONELINESS MISUSES COMMUNITY

Let him who cannot be alone beware of community. He will
only do harm to himself and to the community. . . . But the
reverse is also true: Let him who is not in community beware of
being alone.

—DIETRICH BONHOEFFER

*"The whole congregation of believers was united as one—one
heart, one mind! They didn't even claim ownership of their
own possessions. No one said, 'That's mine; you can't have it.'
They shared everything."*

—ACTS 4:32 (MSG)

The Big Idea: The loneliness God built inside us is meant
to drive us into an intimate relationship with him and into a deep
commitment to each other. But the idea that we long to belong
does not mean we are meant to join a group of believers simply for
social reasons or because we are afraid of being alone.

We belong to the Body of Christ, so think about this: A foot wouldn't join the Body just to avoid being lonely. In fact, when the foot joins the Body, it is expected to be a functioning part of the Body, interconnected with *and fully committed* to the other parts. And in joining the Body, the foot submits to the head, Jesus, who connects us all together in authentic, transparent Christian fellowship.

The thing is, when we join the Body, we are called to a commitment to each other that sweeps us past superficial friendships and beyond once-a-week Bible studies.

Bonhoeffer says if you join the Christ-community just because you fear your loneliness, you will not only be a danger to yourself, but also to the community. "Alone you stood before God when he called you; alone you had to answer that call," Bonhoeffer says. "You cannot escape from yourself; for God has singled you out. If you refuse to be alone you are rejecting Christ's call to you, and you can have no part in the community of those who are called."

But the opposite is also true, Bonhoeffer says: "Let him who is not in community beware of being alone. Into the community you were called, the call was not meant for you alone . . . ." We are called into community in order to struggle and pray together, to bear each others burdens. If we reject Christian community, then we are rejecting the call of Christ, and our solitude becomes harmful to us.

To explain it another way, we must come before God alone to confess our sins, but by confessing our sins and submitting to Christ, we are able to enter the Body of Christ, where we live in union with Jesus and with one another: *"Father! May they be in us, just as you are in me and I am in you. May they be one, so that the world will believe that you sent me"* (John 17:21 TEV).

- Committing to each other in Christian fellowship requires that we lay down our demands that life be lived on our terms. This requires a supernatural shift because, even in our congregations, we've been taught to serve according to what is convenient for us or what interests us. Being in Christian community breaks us of our selfishness.

- Committing to each other in Christian fellowship requires that we love one another no matter what. The apostle John says, *"Love means doing what God has commanded us, and he has commanded us to love one another"* (2 John 1:6 NLT). Since God loves us when we are at our worst, we must love one another even when some of us aren't very lovable (Romans 5:8).

- Committing to each other in Christian fellowship requires we be there for one another. The writer of Hebrews says, *"Let us not give up meeting together, as some are in the habit of doing, but encouraging one another—and all the more as you see the Day approaching"* (Hebrews 10:25 NIV).

Jesus is . . .

Jesus shows us what love is.

To be like Jesus . . .

"Love is made perfect in us in order that we may have courage on the Judgment Day; and we will have it because our life in this world is the same as Christ's. There is no fear in love; perfect love drives out all fear. So then, love has not been made perfect in anyone who is afraid, because fear has to do with punishment" (1 John 4:16-18 TEV).

Scripture:

"The whole congregation of believers was united as one—one heart, one mind! They didn't even claim ownership of their own possessions. No one said, 'That's mine; you can't have it.' They shared everything." (Acts 4:32 MSG)

Questions:

Why do you think Christian fellowship requires an extraordinary commitment to each other? How do you think we can show our commitment to each other?

CHAPTER 16

THE DAY ALONE: SOLITUDE AND SILENCE

Silence is nothing else but waiting for God's Word and coming from God's Word with a blessing. But everybody knows that this is something that needs to be practiced and learned, in these days when talkativeness prevails.

—DIETRICH BONHOEFFER

"Find a quiet, secluded place so you won't be tempted to role-play before God. Just be there as simply and honestly as you can manage. The focus will shift from you to God, and you will begin to sense his grace."

—MATTHEW 6:6 (MSG)

The Big Idea: Bonhoeffer says we need to set aside time every morning for Scripture meditation, prayer, and intercession. In this solitude and silence we develop our oneness with God and our intimacy with him influences the rest of our day.

We need to spend time with God in order to remain intimate with God. Our intimacy with him gives us the confidence and courage to develop intimacy with those in the Body of Christ.

Jesus understood the importance of this and the Bible tells us, *"Jesus often withdrew to lonely places and prayed"* (Luke 5:16 NIV). He didn't just do this every once in a while; it was a habit with him. Bonhoeffer says we need to do this every day in order to hear from the Word, that our "silence before the Word leads to right hearing and thus also to right speaking of the Word of God at the right time."

Bonhoeffer notes, "Silence is the simple stillness of the individual under the Word of God. We are silent before hearing the Word because our thoughts are already directed to the Word, as a child is quiet when he enters his father's room. We are silent after hearing the Word because the Word is still speaking and dwelling within us. We are silent at the beginning of the day because God should have the first word, and we are silent before going to sleep because the last word also belongs to God."

King David teaches us that there are three things to do when we wait in silence before God:

- Wait quietly—*"Let all that I am wait quietly before God, for my hope is in him"* (Psalm 62:5 NLT).
- Wait patiently—*"Be still in the presence of the Lord, and wait patiently for him to act"* (Psalm 37:7a NLT).
- Wait expectantly—*"I wait expectantly, trusting God to help, for he has promised"* (Psalm 130:5 LB). And this is important: you must expect to hear from God.

Jesus is . . .

"Jesus often withdrew to lonely places and prayed" (Luke 5:16 NIV).

To be like Jesus . . .

We meditate before the Word in order to hear from the Word. Bonhoeffer says our "silence before the Word leads to right hearing and thus also to right speaking of the Word of God at the right time."

Scripture:

"Find a quiet, secluded place so you won't be tempted to role-play before God. Just be there as simply and honestly as you can manage. The focus will shift from you to God, and you will begin to sense his grace." (Matthew 6:6 MSG)

Questions:

Where can you establish a special place to have a quiet time with God? Why is it difficult to wait silently for God? Why is it important to expect to hear from God?

CHAPTER 17

THE DAY ALONE: MEDITATION

[Meditation] lets us be alone with the Word. And in so doing it gives us solid ground on which to stand and clear directions as to the steps we must take.

—Dietrich Bonhoeffer

"How happy is the man who does not follow the advice of the wicked or take the path of sinners or join a group of mockers! Instead, his delight is in the LORD's instruction, and he meditates on it day and night. He is like a tree planted beside streams of water that bears its fruit in season and whose leaf does not wither. Whatever he does prospers."

—Psalm 1:1-3 (HCSB)

The Big Idea: Bonhoeffer says we need to set aside time every morning for Scripture meditation, prayer, and intercession. In private meditation, Bonhoeffer says we read God's Word as God's Word for us, not asking what the text has to say to other people, but waiting for God's Word to us.

—∿∿—

Meditation is not some mystical experience that we should fear; rather, it is simply thinking seriously about God's Word. Bonhoeffer says it takes us into the "unfathomable depths of a particular sentence and word," so that we *may have the power to understand how broad and long, how high and deep, is Christ's love*" (Ephesians 3:18 TEV).

"In our meditation we ponder the chosen text on the strength of the promise that it has something utterly personal to say to us for this day and for our Christian life, that it is not only God's Word for the Church, but also God's Word for us individually," Bonhoeffer says. "We expose ourselves to the specific word until it addresses us personally."

When we meditate, we're not just idly waiting; we're waiting in faith, knowing God will keep his promise to speak to us through his Word. Bonhoeffer says this is why we should begin our meditation by asking God to reveal his Word to us.

God may direct us to meditate on one sentence or one word. Bonhoeffer says our thoughts in meditation may be phrases and not complete sentences. And we don't have to start each meditation with a new idea. God may direct us to ponder on something for a while, like Mary who *remembered all these things and thought deeply about them*" the night the shepherds came to see baby Jesus (Luke 2:19 TEV).

Bonhoeffer says God's Word, planted in meditation, "strives to stir us, to work and operate in us, so that we shall not get away from it the whole day long. Then it will do its work in us, often without our being conscious of it." We shouldn't expect to always have extraordinary experiences in meditation. They can happen, but God's Word is still at work even when we feel spiritually dry, even when we struggle to meditate. In fact, Bonhoeffer notes that focusing on an "experience" in meditation will only lead us back into "self-centered introspection," where we make "illicit claims upon God" to always match our fantasy of what is "elevating and fruitful."

Here is what Bonhoeffer believed to be "the fundamental rule of all meditation. If you seek God alone, you will gain happiness: that is its promise." The Bible teaches, "*Whoever looks intently into the perfect law that gives freedom, and continues in it, not forgetting what they have heard, but doing it—they will be blessed in what they do*" (James 1:25 NIV).

Jesus is . . .

"*Love the Lord your God with all your heart, with all your soul, and with all your mind*" (Matthew 22:37 TEV).

To be like Jesus . . .

We meditate so that Jesus, from his glorious, unlimited resources will empower us with inner strength through his Spirit. And so our roots will grow down into God's love, keeping us strong. And so we have the power to understand how wide, how long, how high, and how deep his love is. And so we will experience the love of Christ, though it is too great to understand fully. Then we will be made complete with all the fullness of life and power that comes from God. (based on Ephesians 3:16-19 NLT)

Scripture:

"*How happy is the man [whose] delight is in the LORD's instruction, and he meditates on it day and night. He is like a tree planted beside streams of water that bears its fruit in season and whose leaf does not wither. Whatever he does prospers. The wicked are not like this; instead, they are like chaff that the wind blows away."* (Psalms 1:1-4 HCSB)

Questions:

Why is it important to wait before God's Word? Why do you think meditation establishes your day? If this is true, how will you do things differently?

CHAPTER 18

THE DAY ALONE: PRAYER

Intercession means no more than to bring our brother into the presence of God, to see him under the Cross of Jesus as a poor human being and sinner in need of grace. Then everything in him that repels us falls away; we see him in all his destitution and need. His need and his sin become so heavy and oppressive that we feel them as our own, and we can do nothing else but pray....

—DIETRICH BONHOEFFER

"The earnest prayer of a righteous person has great power and produces wonderful results. Elijah was as human as we are, and yet when he prayed earnestly that no rain would fall, none fell for three and a half years! Then, when he prayed again, the sky sent down rain and the earth began to yield its crops."

—JAMES 5:16B-18 (NLT)

The Big Idea: Bonhoeffer says we need to set aside time every morning for Scripture meditation, prayer, and intercession.

Meditating on Scripture leads to prayer and praying the Word keeps us from becoming "the victims of our own emptiness."

—⁓—

In prayer we receive God's Word and follow it to where God leads, applying it in the details of our lives, in the tasks that we do, in the decisions that we make, and to face-up to our sins and temptations.

We can talk to God about anything and everything, confident that he is interested in the details of our lives. We can boldly go where only those in Christ can go, into the throne room of grace and into the presence of our loving Father. And there we can be certain he will hear our words even as he fulfills the promises of his Word.

We close the door to outside distractions and open our lives before God. We allow him to be the source of all our hopes, but Bonhoeffer notes we must also be ready to go and do what he tells us to go and do. We let God prioritize our day. We listen as he directs us away from sin and temptation. We draw from him the strength to do our work. And we allow him to stretch our faith and mature us into the image of Christ.

Otherwise, we'll just be operating out of sync with him all day, which means we're also out of sync with Jesus and the Body of Christ.

Our prayers reveal our faith in Jesus. When we obediently trust that God hears our prayers, we can watch expectantly for his answer. And when we see him answer, our faith will mature because we see he is trustworthy to keep his promises. In addition, Bonhoeffer says when our prayers conform to the Word of God, we know they are heard and answered because we join the prayers of Jesus, who is already interceding for us.

Bonhoeffer says:

- We must learn to quietly center ourselves on God, peacefully, without agitation and anxiety.
- We may experience wandering thoughts, but one way to handle these is to incorporate them into our prayers, allowing the Spirit to guide us back. We are learning to discipline our thoughts and to concentrate on what God puts before us.
- We learn to hope in the Lord with confident expectation. We trust God even when the answer to our prayers seems a long way off.

Jesus is . . .

Jesus prayed because he wanted to remain intimate with the Father, but he also prayed because he knew God was listening and that his prayers would be answered. He understood his prayers were important.

To be like Jesus . . .

We pray, not only to be intimate with the Father, but also because our prayers bring us into alignment with the Father. Our prayers are important. God listens and God answers. He responds to our needs and he paves the path before us now and forever (Psalm 18:36).

Scripture:

"The earnest prayer of a righteous person has great power and produces wonderful results. Elijah was as human as we are, and yet when he prayed earnestly that no rain would fall, none fell for three

and a half years! Then, when he prayed again, the sky sent down rain and the earth began to yield its crops." (James 5:16b-18 NLT)

Questions:

Why do you think our faith in God is revealed through our prayers? How do you think our prayers align us with God's agenda? Have you ever thought that your prayers can be as effective as Elijah's?

CHAPTER 19

THE DAY ALONE: INTERCESSION

Intercessory prayer is the purifying bath into which the individual and the fellowship must enter every day.

—DIETRICH BONHOEFFER

"In the same way, prayer is essential in this ongoing warfare. Pray hard and long. Pray for your brothers and sisters. Keep your eyes open. Keep each other's spirits up so that no one falls behind or drops out."

—EPHESIANS 6:18 (MSG)

The Big Idea: Bonhoeffer says we need to set aside time every morning for Scripture meditation, prayer, and intercession. Through intercession, we not only provide the *service of prayer* for one another, we also become more like Jesus, who continually intercedes for us before God.

———

Intercession brings the needs of others before God, but it is also a *cleansing agent* that frees *"us from the petty tyrannies of each other"*

(Romans 14:9 MSG). When we plead before God for one another each day, it becomes difficult to remain focused on how others have wronged us or even annoyed us.

When we pray for others, we begin to see them under the cross of Jesus, reminding us *"our old way of life was nailed to the Cross with Christ, a decisive end to that sin-miserable life—no longer at sin's every beck and call! What we believe is this: If we get included in Christ's sin-conquering death, we also get included in his life-saving resurrection"* (Romans 6:6b-8 MSG).

This makes us less likely to judge one another because we're reminded that we are all struggling in some area to put aside the desires of a sinful nature in order to pursue our new life in Christ (Galatians 5:19-21).

The Holy Spirit works within us, helping us put aside the very thing that bothers us about others, and our daily prayers join us with the work of God. In fact, the reason God gives us discernment about a weakness or a fault in another believer is so we will bring the issue before God, praying on behalf of our brother or sister.

We misuse the gift of discernment when we use it in a self-centered manner, such as pointing a finger at someone else. If we spent as much time in intercessory prayer for others as we do complaining about others, how would that change the life of our community? How would that change us?

We pray for others like Jesus would pray for them, covering and protecting them, lifting them before the Father (Romans 8:34).

Bonhoeffer says, "Intercession means no more than to bring our brother into the presence of God, to see him under the Cross of Jesus as a poor human being and sinner in need of grace. Then everything in him that repels us falls away; we see him in all his destitution and need. His need and his sin become so heavy and oppressive that we feel them as our own, and we can do nothing else but pray."

Bonhoeffer says intercession:

- Should not be "general and vague" but specific.
- Shows we have learned to be faithful in "the things of daily life," proving we can be trusted for greater things.
- Requires time, but it is a duty that serves God and serves others, and so no time spent is wasted.

There is a difference between being an intercessor for others and trying to be a mediator for them. We do not connect anyone to God; only Jesus connects them to God. But Jesus calls us to carry each other to God in prayer (Galatians 6:2).

Jesus is . . .

Jesus valued his time with the Father and kept it regardless of what was going on around him.

To be like Jesus . . .

We must value our time with the Father and keep it regardless of what is going on around us. Bonhoeffer says, "We have a right to this time, even prior to the claims of other people, and we may insist upon having it as a completely undisturbed quiet time despite all external difficulties."

Scripture:

"In the same way, prayer is essential in this ongoing warfare. Pray hard and long. Pray for your brothers and sisters. Keep your eyes open. Keep each other's spirits up so that no one falls behind or drops out." (Ephesians 6:18 MSG)

Questions:

How have you interceded for someone in the past and how did you see God answer your prayer? What does Paul mean when he says, *"In the same way, prayer is essential in this ongoing warfare"*? (Ephesians 6:18a MSG).

CHAPTER 20

THE TEST OF MEDITATION

Every day brings to the Christian many hours in which he will be alone in an unchristian environment. These are the times of testing. This is the test of true meditation and true Christian community.

—Dietrich Bonhoeffer

And the peace of God, which transcends all understanding, will guard your hearts and your minds in Christ Jesus.

—Philippians 4:7 (NIV)

The Big Idea: After meditating before God in the morning, we will be tested throughout the day. Bonhoeffer says this will reveal whether or not our time with God "lodged the Word of God so securely and deeply" in our heart that it holds and fortifies us, moving us "to active love, to obedience, to good works."

⁓

When we head into the day, we quickly see if our time spent with God in the morning sticks or slips away. Are we walking in the reality of God's grace or are we living in a fantasy where we live as if we are independent from God? Is God just our morning lift and encouragement or does he get the last word on everything we do throughout the day?

And what about the influence of our fellowship on each of us? Bonhoeffer asks what our journey into the workaday world will reveal: Have we built up one another so that each of us is "free, strong, and mature" or have we pulled each other down, leaving us "weak and dependent"?

We're called to carry honesty, humility, authenticity, grace, love, and obedience into our daily environment. And because the Holy Spirit energizes us, we have the ability to respond to problems in a different way than those who are not connected to the divine nature. We can respond to difficulties like people from the kingdom of heaven, not like those seemingly abandoned by God or unaware of God.

In addition, we are capable, if we choose, to confront temptation in a mature manner, obediently trusting that God will not send us anything stronger than we can handle and obediently taking thoughts captive before they bloom into fully formed sin.

Bonhoeffer says, "Every act of self-control of the Christian is also a service to the fellowship." This is another reminder that our sin is never contained just to ourselves; it always comes with collateral damage, hurting those around us in ways we can see and ways we cannot. The effects of sin ripple through the spiritual realm as well as the physical.

Bonhoeffer says, "There is no sin in thought, word, or deed, no matter how personal or secret, that does not inflict injury upon the whole fellowship. An element of sickness gets into the body; perhaps nobody knows where it comes from or in what member it has lodged, but the body is infected."

As we've already noted, the Bible says, *"We are part of the body of Christ and spiritually one with the Lord"* (1 Corinthians 6:15 TEV). This means, Bonhoeffer says, "We are members of a body, not only when we choose to be, but in our whole existence. Every member serves the whole body, either to its health or to its destruction. This is no mere theory; it is a spiritual reality. And the Christian community has often experienced its effects with disturbing clarity, sometimes destructively and sometimes fortunately."

But if we allow the Holy Spirit to do his work, the test of our meditation will reveal that our hearts and minds are guarded by the peace of God (Philippians 4:7). The apostle Paul's language implies that God's peace, like a military unit, will be garrisoned in our hearts and minds, providing an ever-present protection from within.

We no longer are limited to external factors to overcome our sin. God is poised to protect us from the inside out, helping us to make smart choices and to flee sin if we're close to being overcome. Our meditation reminds us not only of the presence of God, but also that he carries us into the workaday world.

Jesus is . . .

Jesus consistently spent time with God in the morning and it strengthened him when he faced temptation. *"Once more, Jesus went away and prayed, 'My Father, if this cup of suffering cannot be taken away unless I drink it, your will be done'"* (Matthew 26:42 TEV).

To be like Jesus . . .

By faithfully meeting God each morning, we can enter the day confident that God is at work in and around us. We can be certain he goes before us and comes behind. *"For from him and through him and to him are all things. To him be the glory forever! Amen"* (Romans 11:36 NIV).

Scripture:

"And the peace of God, which transcends all understanding, will guard your hearts and your minds in Christ Jesus." (Philippians 4:7 NIV)

Questions:

Jesus took the time to meditate before God. Why do you think we often have trouble making time in the morning to spend with God? How does knowing your sin will affect others change your thoughts about sin? How will it change your behavior?

CHAPTER 21

RANKING RIVALS WHILE IGNORING GOD

There is no time to lose here, for from the first moment when a man meets another person he is looking for a strategic position he can assume and hold over against that person. There are strong persons and weak ones. If a man is not strong, he immediately claims the right of the weak as his own and uses it against the strong. There are gifted and ungifted persons, simple people and difficult people, devout and less devout, the sociable and the solitary.

—DIETRICH BONHOEFFER

"That means we will not compare ourselves with each other as if one of us were better and another worse. We have far more interesting things to do with our lives. Each of us is an original."

—GALATIANS 5:26 (MSG)

The Big Idea: One of the things we have to give up when we enter Christian fellowship is the way we judge and rank each other.

We have a tendency to consign people to certain roles and then we refuse to release them from those roles. It is one way we try to control those around us.

We rank one another according to who we think is most spiritual and who is least, including thinking of ourselves as more spiritually mature than the next. But the truth is we have no idea what sin is nestled in another's heart and, often, we are unable to see how Jesus is transforming someone before our blind eyes.

We may judge someone to be the bold, articulate spokesman while tagging another as shy and nervous. But God may not want someone with a polished presence to carry out an assignment, so he will send the shy to show that he can speak through anyone.

Bonhoeffer says this is "the struggle of the natural man for self-justification. He finds it only in comparing himself with others, in condemning and judging others. Self-justification and judging others go together, as justification by grace and serving others go together."

When the disciples began to argue over who was the greatest, Jesus told them that the least would become the greatest (Luke 9:46-48). He taught that the one who serves is the greatest, that even he did not come to be served, but to serve.

The apostle Paul explained, "*Among those who belong to Christ, everything connected with getting our own way and mindlessly responding to what everyone else calls necessities is killed off for good—crucified. Since this is the kind of life we have chosen, the life of the Spirit, let us make sure that we do not just hold it as an idea in our heads or a sentiment in our hearts, but work out its implications in every detail of our lives. That means we will not compare ourselves with each other as if one of us were better and another worse. We have far more interesting things to do with our lives. Each of us is an original"* (Galatians 5:24-26 MSG).

Paul calls us back to Jesus, the one who connects us to one another, the one who gives us new life. In Christ, we find the grace to set aside our agenda for personal advancement and the power to advance the best interests of one another. We're able to see the true value of one another and affirm how much each of us is worth.

Bonhoeffer says, "I can never know beforehand how God's image should appear in others. That image always manifests a completely new and unique form that comes solely from God's free and sovereign creation. To me the sight may seem strange, even ungodly. But God creates every man in the likeness of His Son, the Crucified."

In other words, *"How do you expect to get anywhere with God when you spend all your time jockeying for position with each other, ranking your rivals and ignoring God?"* (John 5:44 MSG).

Bonhoeffer adds, "Every Christian community must realize that not only do the weak need the strong, but also that the strong cannot exist without the weak. The elimination of the weak is the death of fellowship."

When we allow others in the community to remain under-valued, not involving them in ministry, not allowing them to use their gifts, we weaken the whole community. Bonhoeffer says, "In a Christian community everything depends upon whether each individual is an indispensable link in a chain. Only when even the smallest link is securely interlocked is the chain unbreakable."

"That means we will not compare ourselves with each other as if one of us were better and another worse. We have far more interesting things to do with our lives. Each of us is an original." (Galatians 5:26 MSG)

Jesus is . . .

Instead of ranking rivals, Jesus looked for opportunities to serve. Jesus *"didn't think so much of himself that he had to cling to the advantages of that status no matter what. Not at all. When the time came, he set aside the privileges of deity and took on the status of a slave, became human!"* (Philippians 2:6-7 MSG).

To be like Jesus . . .

"Think of yourselves the way Christ Jesus thought of himself" (Philippians 2:5 MSG). Jesus sets us free from the tyranny of comparing ourselves to one another. We are all equal in Christ. When we start comparing ourselves to each other, we shift back to measuring life by the law—who scores highest, who scores lowest.

Scripture:

"If you've gotten anything at all out of following Christ, if his love has made any difference in your life, if being in a community of the Spirit means anything to you, if you have a heart, if you care—then do me a favor: Agree with each other, love each other, be deep-spirited friends. Don't push your way to the front; don't sweet-talk your way to the top. Put yourself aside, and help others get ahead. Don't be obsessed with getting your own advantage. Forget yourselves long enough to lend a helping hand." (Philippians 2:1-4 MSG)

Questions:

Why do you think we tend to compare ourselves to one another? Why do you think we try to get advantage over others, even in a Christian fellowship? The apostle Paul says we shouldn't compare ourselves to each other because "we have far more interesting things to do with our lives. Each of us is an original" (Galatians 5:26 MSG). What do you think he means?

CHAPTER 22

THE MINISTRY OF SPEAKING THE TRUTH IN LOVE

God did not make this person as I would have made him. He did not give him to me as a brother for me to dominate and control, but in order that I might find above him the Creator.

—DIETRICH BONHOEFFER

"... we will grow to become in every respect the mature body of him who is the head, that is, Christ."

—EPHESIANS 4:15 (NIV)

The Big Idea: When we speak the truth in love, we bring out the best in one another. We are called to encourage and confront each other in the Body of Christ; in fact, it is a service we are expected to provide so we can all mature into the image of Jesus. We're to speak words empowered by Jesus, not influenced by our own opinions or motives.

———

Imagine how your life would change if you committed to never talking about another person's faults unless that person was included in the conversation? How would that change your family? Your workplace? Your small group?

Dietrich Bonhoeffer suggests we employ this strategy in our Life Together: "Thus it must be a decisive rule of every Christian fellowship—to speak about a brother covertly is forbidden, even under the cloak of help and good will; for it is precisely in this guise that the spirit of hatred among brothers always creeps in when it is seeking to create mischief."

Of course, such a strategy could be stifling if we stuffed our frustrations until they erupted, Vesuvius-like, into angry accusations and self-righteous indignation.

But what if, instead, we allowed such a strategy to provoke us into greater maturity? What if we learned to speak the truth in love, helping one another to become more like Jesus?

The apostle Paul says, *"God wants us to grow up, to know the whole truth and tell it in love—like Christ in everything. We take our lead from Christ, who is the source of everything we do. He keeps us in step with each other. His very breath and blood flow through us, nourishing us so that we will grow up healthy in God, robust in love"* (Ephesians 4:15-16 MSG).

Being healthy in God means we speak the truth to one another; we say what needs to be said—but we say it rooted in Christ's love that flows through us. In a sense, *"It is no longer I who speak, but it is Christ who speaks through me"* (based on Galatians 2:20).

The truth we speak is not based on our own opinions or our anger or our motives or even our own perceptions. We speak past the temporary, the annoying, the inconvenient, speaking, instead, to the eternal (2 Corinthians 4:18).

When we do this, Bonhoeffer says, we allow one another the freedom to be who God created us to be. We are able to see, shining above one another, "the richness of God's creative glory."

Because we carry the Word within us, our rule is to not *"use harmful words, but only helpful words, the kind that build up and provide what is needed, so that what you say will do good to those who hear you"* (Ephesians 4:29 TEV).

And this keeps our speech robust with love. We don't demand and we don't try to control others through our words. Think about this: in heaven there will be no criticism, fault-finding, or mean-spirited judgment. We will speak in God's language of love instead of Satan's language of insult and put-down.

And if Satan will have no voice in eternity, he shouldn't have a voice in us now.

Jesus is . . .

Jesus says he only spoke what the Father instructed him to say. (John 8:28) This means he listened carefully to God and then spoke in a way that matched God's agenda. In other words, he didn't just pop-off with his opinion; he carefully considered the words he would use.

To be like Jesus . . .

"We do not speak in words taught by human wisdom, but in words taught by the Spirit, as we explain spiritual truths to those who have the Spirit. . . . As the scripture says, 'Who knows the mind of the Lord? Who is able to give him advice?' We, however, have the mind of Christ" (1 Corinthians 2:13, 16 TEV).

Scripture:

"Our counsel is that you warn the freeloaders to get a move on. Gently encourage the stragglers, and reach out for the exhausted, pulling them to their feet. Be patient with each person, attentive to individual needs. And be careful that when you get on each other's nerves you don't snap at each other. Look for the best in each other, and always do your best to bring it out." (1 Thessalonians 5:14-15 MSG)

Questions:

Imagine how your life would change if you committed to never talking about another person's faults unless that person was included in the conversation. How would that change your family? Your workplace? Your small group?

CHAPTER 23

THE MINISTRY OF MEEKNESS

He who would learn to serve must first learn to think little of himself.

—DIETRICH BONHOEFFER

"And all of you must put on the apron of humility, to serve one another; for the scripture says, 'God resists the proud, but shows favor to the humble.' Humble yourselves, then, under God's mighty hand, so that he will lift you up in his own good time."

—1 PETER 5:5B-6 (TEV)

The Big Idea: Meekness means we submit to God and then draw our strength and authority from him. Grabbing for power is the opposite of Christ-likeness. When we are meek we place the interests of others above our own, working as hard or harder for their growth than we would for our own.

—∿∿—

We tend to think of meekness as a synonym for weakness, or a form of childlike vulnerability. But tender Jesus, meek and mild, slips into our midst with a different definition.

Jesus shows us that meekness is actually a faithful and sacrificial submission to the Heavenly Father's plan. When Jesus voluntarily removed his heavenly cloak, he showed us that he trusted the Father to make good on all his promises.

Jesus says the meek will inherit the earth and that means assertiveness training will put us in last place in the kingdom of heaven: *"Whoever wants to be first must place himself last of all and be the servant of all"* (Mark 9:35 TEV).

Like Jesus, those who are meek focus on giving and not getting; they entrust rather than take. Like Jesus, those who are meek trade their privileges and status in order to serve and sacrifice for others.

In meekness, Jesus set aside any concern for personal comfort and honor in order to carry his concern for the human race on his shoulders. In meekness, Jesus established that God's power is never received by seizing or grabbing—but in spending and being spent for others (Philippians 2:7).

How do we get to meekness? Bonhoeffer says, "He who would learn to serve must first learn to think little of himself." This means we live within the costly grace of God, remembering we have been forgiven of our sins and accepted into the Body of Christ through the blood of Jesus Christ, not by anything we have done.

The apostle Paul says, *"The only accurate way to understand ourselves is by what God is and by what he does for us, not by what we are and what we do for him"* (Romans 12:3b MSG). We cannot serve others in meekness if we think their sins are somehow worse than our own.

Jesus showed us that the greatest power comes when, in meekness, we submit to God. *"Jesus knew that the Father had given him complete power; he knew that he had come from God and was going to God"* (John 13:3 TEV). Because Jesus knew where he was from and where he was going, *"he rose from the table, took off his outer garment, and tied a towel around his waist"* (John 13:4 TEV). Meekness is not afraid to be mistaken for a servant because meekness is about serving others.

Because Jesus was meek:

- He wasn't concerned about what others thought of him. *"I'm not interested in crowd approval. And do you know why? Because I know you and your crowds. I know that love, especially God's love, is not on your working agenda. I came with the authority of my Father, and you either dismiss me or avoid me"* (John 5:41-43a MSG). And so Jesus was not afraid to hang out with sinners.
- He wouldn't allow anyone to distract him from his mission. *"As the time approached for him to be taken up to heaven, Jesus resolutely set out for Jerusalem"* (Luke 9:51 NIV). One translation says he set his face like flint toward Jerusalem.

Bonhoeffer says, "One who seeks his own honor is no longer seeking God and his neighbor. What does it matter if I suffer injustice? Would I not have deserved even worse punishment from God, if He had not dealt with me according to His mercy?"

Jesus is . . .

"Think of yourselves the way Christ Jesus thought of himself. He had equal status with God but didn't think so much of himself that he had to cling to the advantages of that status no matter what. Not at all. When the time came, he set aside the privileges of deity and took on the status of a slave, became human! Having become human,

he stayed human. It was an incredibly humbling process. He didn't claim special privileges. Instead, he lived a selfless, obedient life and then died a selfless, obedient death—and the worst kind of death at that: a crucifixion" Philippians 2:5-8 (MSG).

To be like Jesus . . .

"Put your self aside, and help others get ahead" (Philippians 2:3b MSG).

Scripture:

"I, your Lord and Teacher, have just washed your feet. You, then, should wash one another's feet. I have set an example for you, so that you will do just what I have done for you." John 13:14-15 (TEV)

Questions:

What does it mean to be confident in God but rooted in humility? What are ways you can *"put your self aside, and help others get ahead"*? (Philippians 2:3 MSG). How will your behavior change now that you understand humility and meekness are tied to your ministry in the Body of Christ?

CHAPTER 24

THE MINISTRY OF LISTENING

We should listen with the ears of God that we may speak the Word of God.

—DIETRICH BONHOEFFER

"And Jesus concluded, 'Listen, then, if you have ears!'"

—MARK 4:9 (TEV)

The Big Idea: The way we listen to others is a reflection of how we listen to God, and listening is the key to deepening our faith. Listening to others is an essential service, or ministry, God tells us to provide to one another.

One of the most extraordinary things about Jesus when he was on earth was the way he consistently listened to the people around him. He took the time to hear what others had to say and he showed genuine interest in their thoughts.

He could have dismissed them or condescended to them. He was, after all, the Word dwelling among us, God in the flesh. He was the King of kings, who gave up his rightful place in heaven in order to rescue us from our sin and bring us home to the Father forever and ever. But instead of being too busy, we see Jesus stopping to ask questions and to listen.

If we want to be like Jesus, we have to learn to listen to one another. Bonhoeffer says our unwillingness to listen to one another reveals a resistance to God: "Anyone who thinks that his time is too valuable to spend keeping quiet will eventually have no time for God and his brother, but only for himself and for his own follies."

Listening is one of the ways we serve others in the Body of Christ. Bonhoeffer says it is also how we learn to love one another: "Just as love to God begins with listening to His Word, so the beginning of love for the brethren is learning to listen to them. It is God's love for us that He not only gives us His Word but also lends us His ear."

We offer our presence and open our ears, listening to the hidden hurts and heartaches, the deepest dreams and desires of one another. We respect others enough to let them get the whole story out before we rush in with an answer (1 Corinthians 1:10).

"There is a kind of listening with half an ear that presumes already to know what the other person has to say," Bonhoeffer says. "It is an impatient, inattentive listening, that despises the brother and is only waiting for a chance to speak and thus get rid of the other person."

Listening requires we be fully present in the present. Jim Elliot, the martyred missionary, phrased it this way: "Wherever you are, be all there." Our focus on the present teaches us to be sensitive to the needs, hurts, likes, dislikes, and even joys of those we live with in visible community.

Jesus shows us how to listen when he talks to the Samaritan woman at the well. She eventually tells the village, *"Come see a man who knew all about the things I did, who knows me inside and out. Do you think this could be the Messiah?' And they went out to see for themselves"* (John 4:29-30 MSG).

Keep in mind that Jesus is not omnipotent; he voluntarily left that ability behind in heaven. But Jesus is in tune with God, listening to the Holy Spirit and listening to the woman's needs.

Contrast that with how the disciples listened: *"Just then his disciples came back. They were shocked. They couldn't believe he was talking with that kind of a woman. No one said what they were all thinking, but their faces showed it. The woman took the hint and left. In her confusion she left her water pot"* (John 4:27-28 MSG).

She felt condemned by the disciples, but she felt accepted by Jesus. We were created to listen, and by listening to others, we prove that we've *"started listening to a new master, one whose commands set you free to live openly in his freedom!"* (Romans 6:17-18 MSG).

Jesus is . . .

Jesus listens because he knows it is one way to show us his love for us. He listens because he wants a relationship with us; he didn't come to bring us a set of rules. Jesus listens because he knows that, through listening, faith is increased: *"To those who listen to my teaching, more understanding will be given, and they will have an abundance of knowledge. But for those who are not listening, even what little understanding they have will be taken away from them"* (Matthew 13:12 NLT).

To be like Jesus . . .

Listening is a Christ-like characteristic, so we must learn to listen to Jesus and to one another. When we listen, we show each other what Jesus looks like: *"Whoever listens to you listens to me; whoever rejects you rejects me; but whoever rejects me rejects him who sent me"* (Luke 10:13-19 NIV).

Scripture:

"But now that you've found you don't have to listen to sin tell you what to do, and have discovered the delight of listening to God telling you, what a surprise! A whole, healed, put-together life right now, with more and more of life on the way!" Romans 6:22-23 (MSG)

Questions:

When someone listens intently to what you have to say, how does that make you feel? If someone half-listens to you, how does that make you feel? Jesus says, in a sense, our faith is increased through listening. Why do you think he says that? How might listening be related to love? How might listening be related to obedience?

CHAPTER 25

THE MINISTRY OF HELPFULNESS

We must be ready to allow ourselves to be interrupted by God. God will be constantly crossing our paths and canceling our plans by sending us people with claims and petitions.

—DIETRICH BONHOEFFER

"Jesus stopped and called them. 'What do you want me to do for you?' he asked them."

—MATTHEW 20:32 (TEV)

The Big Idea: The second service we should offer one another is helpfulness. We're to become like the Good Samaritan, always ready to stop for someone in need. Our priority is always God's agenda, not our own. If we do not serve one another, then our community is not Christian.

Jesus stopped. He stopped when people needed his help, when they needed his comfort, when they needed his protection, when they needed an answer to a perplexing problem.

Even though Jesus was on an urgent and vital mission, he took time to stop because he saw the interruptions in his life as divine opportunities to show God's love to people in desperate need.

And his example makes it pretty difficult for us to think, say, or act like we are too busy to stop and serve those around us. Bonhoeffer rightly notes that someone who worries about the loss of time that simple "acts of helpfulness entail is usually taking the importance of his own career too solemnly."

We become, Bonhoeffer says, like the priest who, perhaps reading his Bible, walked by the man beset by thieves on road to Jericho. He says when we do this, "we pass by the visible sign of the Cross" that God has placed in our path "to show us that, not our way, but God's way must be done."

Bonhoeffer says, "It is a strange fact that Christians and even ministers frequently consider their work so important and urgent that they will allow nothing to disturb them." He says they think they are doing God a service in this, when they are actually showing contempt for God's call that we live a life of service and sacrifice.

"But it is part of the discipline of humility that we must not spare our hand where it can perform a service and that we do not assume that our schedule is our own to manage, but allow it to be arranged by God," says Bonhoeffer.

Listen to the apostle John: *"If you see some brother or sister in need and have the means to do something about it but turn a cold shoulder and do nothing, what happens to God's love? It disappears. **And you made it disappear**"* (1 John 3:17 MSG, emphasis added).

Jesus is . . .

Jesus says, *"For even the Son of Man came not to be served but to serve others and to give his life as a ransom for many"* (Matthew 20:28 NLT).

To be like Jesus . . .

Jesus says, *"But among you it will be different. Whoever wants to be a leader among you must be your servant, and whoever wants to be first among you must become your slave."* (Matthew 20:26-27 NLT) In addition, the apostle Paul says you become like Jesus when you *"use your freedom to serve one another in love. For the whole law can be summed up in this one command: 'Love your neighbor as yourself'"* (Galatians 5:13b-14 NLT).

Scripture:

"What is important is faith expressing itself in love." Galatians 5:6 (NIV)

Questions:

Paul's phrase, "faith expressing itself in love," suggests our acts of service not only reveal our love for one another; they also require faith. Why would an act of service require faith? What kind of service might require faith? How would simply setting aside your agenda to stop and help someone require faith?

CHAPTER 26

THE MINISTRY OF BEARING

The brother is a burden to the Christian, precisely because he is a Christian.

—DIETRICH BONHOEFFER

"Help carry one another's burdens, and in this way you will obey the law of Christ."

—GALATIANS 6:2 (TEV)

The Big Idea: Jesus wants us to understand that bearing the burdens of one another is a required service in the Body of Christ. We're connected together through Jesus and so any burden that threatens to overwhelm one of us should be a burden to all of us.

We are called to bear one another's burdens, even if that means we carry someone's burden for a while, like Simon from Cyrene shouldered the heavy wooden cross for Jesus as Jesus carried our sins on his shoulder up the hill called Calvary (Mark 15:21).

Bonhoeffer says, "It is only when he is a burden that another person is really a brother and not merely an object to be manipulated. The burden of men was so heavy for God Himself that He had to endure the Cross."

Isaiah says Jesus *"endured the suffering that should have been ours, the pain that we should have borne.... Because of our sins he was wounded, beaten because of the evil we did. We are healed by the punishment he suffered, made whole by the blows he received"* (Isaiah 53:4-5 TEV).

The apostle Paul says we complete the "law of Christ" when we help each other face the troubles and trials of life (Galatians 6:2).

By sharing one another's burdens, the Body of Christ becomes a powerful setting to learn compassion, another characteristic we must develop on our way to becoming living images of Jesus Christ. We come to see that those who are a burden—who we may label weak—are the very things that make us a community. They teach us how to offer sacrificial service to others and they help us understand that, bearing the cost so that others may go free, is one of the ways we develop the characteristics of Jesus: *"The Lord is close to the brokenhearted and saves those who are crushed in spirit"* (Psalm 34:18 NIV).

Bonhoeffer says, "To cherish no contempt for the sinner but rather to prize the privilege of bearing him means not to have to give him up as lost, to be able to accept him, to preserve fellowship with him through forgiveness." We are called to be *"tolerant with one another,"* doing our best to *"preserve the unity which the Spirit gives by means of the peace that binds [us] together"* (Ephesians 4:2-3 TEV).

The apostle Paul adds, *"There is one body and one Spirit, just as there is one hope to which God has called you. There is one Lord, one faith, one baptism; there is one God and Father of all people, who is Lord of all, works through all, and is in all"* (Ephesians 4:4-6 TEV).

Bonhoeffer says, "As Christ bore and received us as sinners so we in his fellowship may bear and receive sinners into the fellowship of Jesus Christ through the forgiving of sins. We may suffer the sins of our brother; we do not need to judge. This is a mercy for the Christian; for when does sin ever occur in the community that he must not examine and blame himself for his own unfaithfulness in prayer and intercession, his lack of brotherly service, of fraternal reproof and encouragement, indeed, for his own personal sin and spiritual laxity, by which he has done injury to himself, the fellowship, and the brethren?"

In Christian community we learn to be ready to help those who need help, as God reveals their needs to us. And then we need to be ready to address the needs and concerns God reveals to us. *"We who are strong ought to bear with the failings of the weak and not to please ourselves. Each of us should please our neighbors for their good, to build them up,"* says the apostle Paul (Romans 15:1–2 NIV).

Paul says further, *"If someone is caught in any kind of wrongdoing, those of you who are spiritual should set him right; but you must do it in a gentle way. And keep an eye on yourselves, so that you will not be tempted, too"* (Galatians 6:1 TEV). Our fellowship is no place for a holier-than-thou attitude because, eventually, we will need others to set us right.

None of us is strong enough to guarantee we will never slip back into living the old, worldly ways, once abandoned for Christ (Romans 14–15; Galatians 6; James 5). We need each other's help to grow in the grace and truth of Christ. The Bible says, *"Two are better off than one, because together they can work more effectively. If one of them falls down, the other can help him up. But if someone is alone and falls, it's just too bad, because there is no one to help him"* (Ecclesiastes 4:9-10 TEV).

Bonhoeffer says, "Since every sin of every member burdens and indicts the whole community, the congregation rejoices, in the midst of all the pain and the burden the brother's sin inflicts, that it has the privilege of bearing and forgiving." He adds, "He who is bearing others knows that he himself is being borne, and only in this strength can he go on bearing."

Jesus is . . .

Jesus willingly bore our sins so that we could be free to follow him to heaven.

To be like Jesus . . .

We're called to bear the sins of others, regardless of the costs. Bearing one another's burdens is one of the ways we become like Jesus.

Scripture:

"Help carry one another's burdens, and in this way you will obey the law of Christ." Galatians 6:2 (TEV)

Questions:

Bonhoeffer says, "If we do not experience others bearing us, then the group we belong to is not Christian." What do you think Bonhoeffer means by this? What do you think about his statement? Bonhoeffer also says, "And if anyone refuses to bear another's burden, then he denies the law of Christ." The law of Christ is that we love one another. How will you do things differently knowing that bearing someone else's burdens reflects your obedience to Jesus?

CHAPTER 27

THE MINISTRY OF PROCLAIMING

We speak to one another on the basis of the help we both need.
We admonish one another to go the way that Christ bids us to
go. We warn one another against the disobedience that is our
common destruction. We are gentle and we are severe with one
another, for we know both God's kindness and God's severity.

—DIETRICH BONHOEFFER

"My friends, if any of you wander away from the truth and
another one brings you back again, remember this: whoever
turns a sinner back from the wrong way will save that
sinner's soul from death and bring about the forgiveness of
many sins."

—JAMES 5:19-20 (TEV)

The Big Idea: Because we are connected to Christ, we
carry the responsibility in our fellowship of believers to speak
the Word to one another. We are a witness of the Holy Spirit's
counsel, of the mind of Christ, and of the wisdom of God, and
Jesus speaks through us in order to keep each other headed in the
right direction.

By speaking the Word to one another, we keep Christ in our con-versations. This is not the kind of proclaiming meant for the pulpit and, when we attempt it that way, we come off as "preachy." Rather, this is speaking to others on behalf of the Word, where Bonhoeffer notes we give "the whole consolation of God, the admonition, the kindness, and the severity of God."

When we speak the Word to one another, Bonhoeffer isn't referring to the sort of superficial, often mindless, verse-dropping we do when we slip into the language of Christian-ese. We come to our brother or sister submitted to the Word, not only saying what Jesus tells us to say, but also reflecting our obedience to Christ in our own behavior. As the apostle Paul says, we come represent-ing Christ, as if *"God is making his appeal through us. We speak for Christ when we plead, 'Come back to God!'"* (2 Corinthians 5:20 NLT).

This means we come actively listening. Not only do we listen to what God wants us to say, allowing the Holy Spirit to give us super-natural discernment, we also listen to those we confront, hearing what they are thinking, like Jesus listens to us, even though we fall short of his expectations.

This means we come in an attitude of humble helpfulness, willing to invest in the life of the one we confront. We come willing to walk with one another even as we warn because, as Bonhoeffer notes, if we come in impatience or the desire to force others to accept the Word, then what we say will be neither liberating nor healing (again, we have to trust the Word is at work, even if we don't see it).

Bonhoeffer asks, "Who wants to be accountable for having been silent when he should have spoken?" In fact, he says it is much easier to speak from the pulpit following an outline than it is to lovingly proclaim the Word to one another in our fellowship, where Paul says our responsibility is to speak *"in the sight of God as those in Christ,"* so that *"everything we do, dear friends, is for your strengthening"* (2 Corinthians 12:19 NIV).

Back at the dawn of man, Cain asked the question, "Am I my brother's keeper?" In Christian community, the answer is "Yes!" You have the responsibility to warn me, if you see me slipping into sin or stumbling in my faith. And I have the responsibility to warn you. God created us to live in community so that, just as *"iron sharpens iron,"* we can push each other toward Christ-like character (Proverbs 27:17).

Although we speak, in Bonhoeffer's term, the severity of God, we do so with redemptive purpose. We call those we rebuke back to the *things above*, pointing them to where we all must remain— under the cross of Christ (Colossians 3:1-4).

The apostle Paul speaks of warning others *"night and day with tears"* (Acts 20:31 NIV). In doing this, we give witness to our commitment to one another, caring enough to confront and to exhort our brothers and sisters to continue in their good fight of faith.

Bonhoeffer says it is inconceivable that we would fail to talk to one another about things that are so significant they have eternal consequences. "If we cannot bring ourselves to utter it," he says, "we shall have to ask ourselves whether we are not still seeing our brother garbed in his human dignity which we are afraid to touch, and thus forgetting the most important thing, that he, too, no matter how old or highly placed or distinguished he may be, is still a man like us, a sinner in crying need of God's grace."

We grant one another true dignity when we confront the sins in others; yet, also remind them that they share in God's grace and glory and that they are God's child. Our commitment to one another is founded on our understanding that each of us, though sinners, are accepted into God's family because of Jesus, and nothing more. This allows us to be candid, free to speak the words Jesus gives us to say.

"We speak to one another on the basis of the help we both need," says Bonhoeffer. "We admonish one another to go the way that Christ bids us to go. We warn one another against the disobedience that is our common destruction. We are gentle and we are severe with one another, for we know both God's kindness and God's severity."

Bonhoeffer suggests that the more open we are to hear the Word spoken to us, "the more free and objective will we be in speaking ourselves." Those who are afraid to be confronted tend to not confront others, or they confront in ways that are destructive to our fellowship.

Bonhoeffer admits confronting one another with the Word is unavoidable in our fellowship because God's Word demands it. "The practice of discipline in the congregation begins in the smallest circles," says Bonhoeffer. "Where defection from God's Word in doctrine or life imperils the family fellowship and with it the whole congregation, the word of admonition and rebuke must be ventured."

He adds, "Nothing can be more cruel than the tenderness that consigns another to his sin. Nothing can be more compassionate than the severe rebuke that calls a brother back from the path of sin." He says we engage in "a ministry of mercy" that leads to genuine fellowship when confronted God's Word.

We serve by speaking the Word, even if it offends, even if, in obedience to God, we must break fellowship with the one we confront. Bonhoeffer says, "We must know that it is not our human love which makes us loyal to the other person, but God's love which breaks its way through to him only through judgment."

It is not our place to force others to change. Bonhoeffer says, "We cannot keep life in what is determined to die." Only God's Word can do that. God puts his Word in our mouths and we are expected to be his messengers. And God says, *"If I announce that someone evil is going to die but you do not warn him to change his ways so that he can save his life, he will die, still a sinner, but I will hold you responsible for his death"* (Ezekiel 3:18 TEV).

Jesus is . . .

When Jesus confronts, his words are not self-seeking or controlling. Rather, they sound like freedom pouring hope into our lives. His eye is on the end-game and his Words are spoken to bring us home to the Father.

To be like Jesus . . .

When we speak the Word to others, we are serving one another. We say what Jesus tells us to say. This allows us to say things with no strings attached, so that what we say is a pure, loving call meant to bring others back to who they truly are *in Christ*. We confront and then we trust the Word will transform. The Word is more powerful than our own demands.

Scripture:

"My friends, if any of you wander away from the truth and another one brings you back again, remember this: whoever turns a sinner back from the wrong way will save that sinner's soul from death and bring about the forgiveness of many sins." James 5:19-20 (TEV)

Questions:

How might we hinder God's Word when we've been told to speak it? Bonhoeffer says when we fail to speak the Word to one another, we are being cruel and unchristian. Why do you think he says that? He also says, "Nothing can be more compassionate than the severe rebuke that calls [another] back from the path of sin." Why would compassion sometimes be confrontational? What keeps you from such a "ministry of mercy."? How is the Word more powerful than our own demands?

CHAPTER 28

THE MINISTRY OF AUTHORITY

Every cult of personality that emphasizes the distinguished qualities, virtues, and talents of another person, even though these be of an altogether spiritual nature, is worldly and has no place in the Christian community; indeed, it poisons the Christian community.

—DIETRICH BONHOEFFER

"This, however, is not the way it is among you. If one of you wants to be great, you must be the servant of the rest; and if one of you wants to be first, you must be the slave of all. For even the Son of Man did not come to be served; he came to serve and to give his life to redeem many people."

—MARK 10:43-45 (TEV)

The Big Idea: The question of trust, which is so closely related to that of authority, is determined by the faithfulness with which a person serves Jesus Christ, never by the extraordinary talents which he or she possesses. We have been given the authority to love one another.

Bonhoeffer notes that New Testament leadership is not defined by "worldly charm" or "brilliant attributes." In fact, the apostle Paul, in effect, tells Timothy, that leadership is as leadership does (1 Timothy 3:1-7). The true test of leadership is in service to others.

Paul says nothing to Timothy about the need to be charismatic or exceptionally gifted, and when Paul writes the Corinthians, he tells them that eloquent speech is never a sign of spiritual leadership, because our words should not come from human wisdom, but should be words *"taught by the Spirit, as we explain spiritual truths to those who have the Spirit"* (1 Corinthians 2:13 TEV). In fact, Paul tells us that love is the only real language a leader needs (1 Corinthians 13:1).

Any authority we have within the Body of Christ comes from our connection to Christ, and the slightest slip away from that basis will undermine the community of Christ, whether it be a leader forgetting "the greatest one among you must be your servant" or a church member insisting on human leadership over and above God (see 1 Samuel 8).

Jesus knew his authority came from God and, as we've discussed, that is why he *got up* from the meal and then *got down* on his knees to wash the feet of his disciples (John 13:4–5). And, then, *"after he had finished washing their feet, he took his robe, put it back on, and went back to his place at the table.*

"You address me as 'Teacher' and 'Master,' and rightly so. That is what I am. So if I, the Master and Teacher, washed your feet, you must now wash each other's feet. I've laid down a pattern for you. What I've done, you do.

"I'm only pointing out the obvious. A servant is not ranked above his master; an employee doesn't give orders to the employer. If

you understand what I'm telling you, act like it—and live a blessed life" (John 13:12-17 MSG).

Jesus teaches us that the only way to lead others is to serve them. Menial was not beneath Jesus. He always placed the needs of others above his own, even as he approached his own death.

Bonhoeffer says the Church needs faithful servants of God, not dazzling personalities. He says, "Pastoral authority can be attained only by the servant of Jesus who seeks no power of his own, who himself is a brother among brothers submitted to the authority of the Word."

The Body will respond to this "simple servant" who is humbly walking toward oneness with Christ. And, if we follow a leader who is walking toward that oneness, then we will be walking toward oneness with Jesus too.

Jesus is . . .

"I, your Lord and Teacher, have just washed your feet. You, then, should wash one another's feet. I have set an example for you, so that you will do just what I have done for you. I am telling you the truth: no slaves are greater than their master, and no messengers are greater than the one who sent them. Now that you know this truth, how happy you will be if you put it into practice!" John 13:12-17 (TEV)

To be like Jesus . . .

Jesus made authority in the fellowship dependent upon brotherly service. Genuine spiritual authority is to be found only where the ministry of hearing, helping, bearing, and proclaiming is carried out.

Scripture:

"The greatest one among you must be your servant. Whoever makes himself great will be humbled, and whoever humbles himself will be made great." Matthew 23:11-12 (TEV)

Questions:

Jesus says, *"I tell you the truth: the Son can do nothing on his own; he does only what he sees his Father doing. What the Father does, the Son also does"* (John 5:19 TEV). What does this teach about leadership in the Body of Christ? We have been given the authority to love one another. What would that type of authority look like?

CHAPTER 29

THE MINISTRY OF CONFESSION AND COMMUNION

The pious fellowship permits no one to be a sinner. So everybody must conceal his sin from himself and from the fellowship. We dare not be sinners. Many Christians are unthinkably horrified when a real sinner is suddenly discovered among the righteous. So we remain alone with our sin, living in lies and hypocrisy. The fact is that we are sinners!

—DIETRICH BONHOEFFER

"Make this your common practice: Confess your sins to each other and pray for each other so that you can live together whole and healed. The prayer of a person living right with God is something powerful to be reckoned with."

—JAMES 5:16 (MSG)

The Big Idea: We must allow one another the freedom to be sinners, rather than hiding behind masks of piety. In Christian community we are free to be honest about our faults and this openness allows us to help one another make the right choices. Otherwise, we leave one another alone in our sins, creating a fellowship of shadows where we never really see each other as flawed people who need Jesus.

—•m•—

We will come back to the theme of confession throughout the remainder of this book, which will serve to remind us that confession is not a small part of Christian faith and fellowship. Confession is foundational to our beliefs. We must confess our sins in order to enter fellowship with Jesus.

And confession is foundational to our fellowship with each other. By keeping our sin lists short, we are able to walk honestly with each other. There is no hidden sin between us and, in the uncommon safety of our transparent fellowship, we are able to strengthen each other toward greater maturity.

Bonhoeffer says that when we hide our sins from one another we are left alone in our sin. And, "he who is alone with his sin is utterly alone."

This is his concern: Do we hide our sins from one another because we sense that our fellowship doesn't really want to deal with the problems of our sins? We'd rather keep relating to each other as good people and ignore the truth that we are sinners saved by grace. And does that lead us to subtly discourage one another from confessing our sins, leaving us alone with them?

Have we created an atmosphere where we are afraid to confess our sins to one another because we think we will find ourselves rejected, judged, and diminished within the community? And, the truth is that our fears are often founded in reality.

And so we wear masks and hide our sins from one another, which actually undermines the intimacy of our community and leaves us still wounded in the dark. Is it any wonder that so many Christian fellowships remain shallow, never developing the deep commitments that are a necessary part of authentic, intimate, and transparent Christian community?

Instead, Bonhoeffer suggests, we have Christian communities filled with seemingly pious people who have forgotten their sinful past and forgotten they are incapable of becoming like Jesus without the bloody sacrifice of Jesus.

He adds, "But it is the grace of the Gospel, which is so hard for the pious to understand, that it confronts us with the truth and says: You are a sinner, a great, desperate sinner; now come, as the sinner that you are, to God who loves you. He wants you as you are; He does not want anything from you, a sacrifice, a work; He wants you alone."

Because of Jesus, we are free to be who God created us to be and we are free to be who we are in Christian community. And that frees our fellowship to help the sinner—each one of us—grow into the fullness of Jesus Christ, our Lord. Bonhoeffer says that we can take that freedom away from each other by refusing to allow others to be real before us, or for us to refuse to be real before others.

Bonhoeffer says God will have none of this pious posing: "He wants to see you as you are, He wants to be gracious to you. You do not have to go on lying to yourself and your brothers, as if you were without sin; you can dare to be a sinner. Thank God for that; He loves the sinner but He hates sin."

And so Jesus gives us the authority to hear the confession of sin and to forgive others in his name (John 20:23). Bonhoeffer says this doesn't mean we have to confess our sins before everyone; rather, we should be accountable to someone in our fellowship.

By giving us the authority to confess to one another and to forgive one another in his name, Jesus made the Body of Christ, and those within our fellowship, a blessing to us. "Now our brother stands in Christ's stead," Bonhoeffer says, and this means we can dare to be who we are and dare to confess our sins. We are all living monuments of the truth and grace of Jesus.

Jesus is . . .

Jesus came to save us from our sins. The last thing he wants is for us to hide them in the shadows. When we do that, we waste the grace he's paid so dearly to provide.

To be like Jesus . . .

Our love for one another should create a safe place, where *"we refuse to wear masks and play games. We don't maneuver and manipulate behind the scenes. And we don't twist God's Word to suit ourselves. Rather, we keep everything we do and say out in the open, the whole truth on display, so that those who want to can see and judge for themselves in the presence of God"* (2 Corinthians 4:2 MSG).

Scripture:

"Make this your common practice: Confess your sins to each other and pray for each other so that you can live together whole and healed. The prayer of a person living right with God is something powerful to be reckoned with." James 5:16 (MSG)

Questions:

What do you think the apostle James means when he says, "confess your sins to one another and pray for one another, so that you will be healed?" (James 5:16 TEV). James also says confession should be our common practice. What would a fellowship that had confession as a common practice look like? What do you think about Bonhoeffer's suggestion that we want to have fellowship with devout Christians but not undevout sinners saved by grace?

CHAPTER 30

In Confession We Break Through to the Community

In confession the break-through to community takes place. Sin demands to have a man by himself. It withdraws him from the community. The more isolated a person is, the more destructive will be the power of sin over him, and the more deeply he becomes involved in it, the more disastrous is his isolation.

—Dietrich Bonhoeffer

"Everyone who does evil hates the light, and will not come into the light for fear that their deeds will be exposed. But whoever lives by the truth comes into the light, so that it may be seen plainly that what they have done has been done in the sight of God."

—John 3:20-21 (NIV)

The Big Idea: Our sin hides in the darkness and whispers to us that it should remain unknown. And when we keep it in the darkness, it spreads within us like a toxin. Because we are a part of the Body of Christ, it seeps into our fellowship, eating away at obedience to Jesus. Even those who are spiritually mature can stumble into sin, and then be tempted by pride to keep it in the dark.

—⁓—

What is sin? Anything that separates you from oneness with God; anything Jesus tells you not to do; anything you wouldn't do, knowing the Holy Spirit is inside you. Sin is anything that pushes God down in your life or out of your life.

Bonhoeffer says, "In confession the light of the Gospel breaks into the darkness and seclusion of the heart." God will not ignore sin; *"he breaks down doors of bronze and smashes iron bars"* because our sin must be brought into the light, (Psalm 107:16 TEV).

By confessing our sin in the presence of another, Bonhoeffer says "the last stronghold of self-justification is abandoned. The sinner surrenders; he gives up all his evil. He gives his heart to God, and he finds the forgiveness of all his sin in the fellowship of Jesus Christ and his brother."

Living in the light lets others see what God is doing in your life, including how far he's brought you from your past and how he's still working with you despite your failures and fears. When we push that part of our life back into the shadows, others are unable to see the redemptive power of Jesus' blood and righteousness (John 3:20–21).

Bonhoeffer notes that when our sin is brought to light, it loses its power over us—and over the community: "It has been revealed and judged as sin." We are no longer alone in our sin and those in our fellowship can now bear the sin with us, strengthening us when we face temptation and helping us to see that our sin reveals a place where we still do not trust God to provide for us or to fulfill his promises to us.

The truth is the fellowship is already bearing our sin, even when it is still in the shadows, because my sin costs you, just as your sin costs me. Consider a father trapped in a pornographic habit. His sin puts him back in rebellion against God as he stubbornly refuses to keep the temptation under the Cross of Jesus. And that affects his walk with Jesus as well as his relationship with others. His sin costs his family in many ways—spiritually, financially, physically—and leaves them vulnerable to attacks from Satan. He is no longer at ease in the fellowship; rather, he is at dis-ease, afraid his sin will be discovered, afraid he will be rejected and shamed.

But we belong to a fellowship of sinners who live within the grace of God, and so we should not fear confession because, in a community submitted to Jesus, confession brings us back into alignment with God and one another. Our confession should, in a community submitted to Jesus, bring us into greater intimacy with each other because we are able to remove the mask that keeps us from truly knowing one another.

Bonhoeffer also says confessing to the whole fellowship is not required. He says we meet the whole congregation in the one person to whom we confess and that person is able to forgive us of our sins in the name of Jesus.

Fellowship with the one opens fellowship with the community because none of us, in hearing confessions from one another and forgiving one another, acts in our own name or from our own authority. Jesus commissions us to this service to one another.

Jesus is . . .

Jesus says, *"I am the light of the world. If you follow me, you won't have to walk in darkness, because you will have the light that leads to life"* (John 8:12 NLT).

To be like Jesus . . .

We must walk in the Light in faithful obedience to the truth that confession reduces the power of our sin. Sin distracts us from the truth that Jesus has given us the freedom to make choices that are pleasing to God. In confession, we reveal, but God heals.

Scripture:

"You are the light of the world. A city situated on a hill cannot be hidden. No one lights a lamp and puts it under a basket, but rather on a lampstand, and it gives light for all who are in the house. In the same way, let your light shine before men, so that they may see your good works and give glory to your Father in heaven." Matthew 5:14-16 (HCSB)

Questions:

Our sin wants to stay in the darkness. How does that connect to Jesus being the Light of the world and telling us to let our light shine before others? Why would you agree or disagree with the following statements:

- Confession deepens our relationships, allowing us to be transparent with one another (Proverbs 24:26).
- Confession keeps our fellowship open and authentic, freeing us to speak the truth in love as we practice remarkable integrity (Ephesians 4:15; Titus 2:7).
- Confession keeps us sensitive to the Holy Spirit's guidance and helps us battle deceptions that corrupt our lives in Christ (John 16:13; 2 Corinthians 10:5).

CHAPTER 31

IN CONFESSION WE BREAK THROUGH TO THE CROSS

The Cross of Jesus Christ destroys all pride. We cannot find the Cross of Jesus if we shrink from going to the place where it is to be found, namely, the public death of the sinner. And we refuse to bear the Cross when we are ashamed to take upon ourselves the shameful death of the sinner in confession.

—DIETRICH BONHOEFFER

"l,.Everyone who does evil hates the light, and will not come into the light for fear that their deeds will be exposed. But whoever lives by the truth comes into the light, so that it may be seen plainly that what they have done has been done in the sight of God."

—JOHN 3:20–21 (NIV)

The Big Idea: Often, when we sin, our pride steps in the way and tells us not to do it. And this just adds the sin of pride to the sin we've stuffed in the shadows. Confessing to another breaks us of our pride because it is painful and humiliating, but it is also the very thing that brings us back to the Cross of Christ, where he suffered pain and humiliation because of our sin.

—~~—

Isn't it funny how we are often more willing to tell our sins to God than we are to confess them to another person? And that is precisely why the Bible teaches us to confess our sins to one another.

It forces us to bring our sin out of the abstract and general into the concrete and specific. It forces us to face the truth that our sin is powerful enough to destroy our fellowship with Jesus and with one another, but it also reminds us that God's grace is greater than our sin, that Jesus shed his blood to bring us back into fellowship with the Father—and to connect us together, accepted in God's beloved family.

Bonhoeffer says, "In the confession of concrete sins the old man dies a painful, shameful death before the eyes of a brother. Because this humiliation is so hard we continually scheme to evade confessing to a brother." Yet, Bonhoeffer adds, Jesus wasn't ashamed to die for us on the cross.

Because the old man dies when we confess to another, we share in the humiliation of the cross and we share in the death of Christ. The apostle Paul says the death of Christ is now *at work in us* so that the life of Christ can be *at work in others* (2 Corinthians 4:8-11).

And this also means we are able to break through to the true fellowship of the cross of Jesus Christ. Bonhoeffer says, "The old man dies, but it is God who has conquered him. Now we share in the resurrection of Christ and eternal life." We learn once again that, "*The God who said, 'Out of darkness the light shall shine!' is the same God who made his light shine in our hearts, to bring us the knowledge of God's glory shining in the face of Christ*" (2 Corinthians 4:6 TEV).

Jesus is . . .

"He was humble and walked the path of obedience all the way to death— his death on the cross" (Philippians 2:8 TEV).

To be like Jesus . . .

"We are pressured in every way but not crushed; we are perplexed but not in despair; we are persecuted but not abandoned; we are struck down but not destroyed. We always carry the death of Jesus in our body, so that the life of Jesus may also be revealed in our body. For we who live are always given over to death because of Jesus, so that Jesus' life may also be revealed in our mortal flesh" (2 Corinthians 4:8-11 HCSB).

Scripture:

"Everyone who does evil hates the light, and will not come into the light for fear that their deeds will be exposed. But whoever lives by the truth comes into the light, so that it may be seen plainly that what they have done has been done in the sight of God." John 3:20–21 (NIV)

Questions:

Why do we often feel more comfortable confessing our sins to God than to another person? What does that say about our approach to confession? Why is it important we confess specific sins rather than confessing in general?

CHAPTER 32

IN CONFESSION WE BREAK
THROUGH TO NEW LIFE

But where there is a break with sin, there is conversion.
Confession is conversion.

—DIETRICH BONHOEFFER

*"All who confess that Jesus is the Son of God have God living
in them, and they live in God. We know how much God
loves us, and we have put our trust in his love. God is love,
and all who live in love live in God, and God lives in them."*

—1 JOHN 4:15-16 (NLT)

The Big Idea: Bonhoeffer says, "Confession is conversion."
We not only confess our sins, but confessing leads to our salvation:
*"If you confess with your mouth, 'Jesus is Lord,' and believe in your
heart that God raised Him from the dead, you will be saved. One
believes with the heart, resulting in righteousness, and one confesses
with the mouth, resulting in salvation"* (Romans 10:9-11 HCSB).

Our breakthrough to new life is through confession: *"This
means that anyone who belongs to Christ has become a new person.
The old life is gone; a new life has begun!"* (2 Corinthians 5:17 NLT).

Bonhoeffer says that confession is discipleship. He says, "As the first disciples left all and followed when Jesus called, so in confession the Christian gives up all and follows." Our life with Christ begins with confession and then confession remains an integral part of our walk with Jesus.

Confession, in fact, is a key to living a victorious Christian life. We learn to forsake our sins and focus on our new life with Jesus. And as we confess, we are stronger in saying no to temptation.

Confession is a reflection of the moment of our salvation. "What happened to us in baptism is bestowed upon us anew in confession," says Bonhoeffer. "We are delivered out of darkness into the kingdom of Jesus Christ. That is joyful news. Confession is the renewal of the joy of baptism." We may face tears in the darkness, *"but joy comes in the morning"* (Psalm 30:5 TEV).

Jesus is . . .

Jesus came to give us new Life.

To be like Jesus . . .

We enter our new life in Christ when we confess our sins and then confess that Jesus is Lord and Savior. The life of Christ works within us to re-create us into the image of Jesus.

Scripture:

"For surely you know that when we were baptized into union with Christ Jesus, we were baptized into union with his death. By our baptism, then, we were buried with him and shared his death, in order that, just as Christ was raised from death by the glorious power of the Father, so also we might live a new life." Romans 6:3-4 (TEV)

Questions:

What does Bonhoeffer mean when he says, "Confession is conversion"? Why is confession a central part of discipleship?

CHAPTER 33

IN CONFESSION WE BREAK THROUGH TO CERTAINTY

And is not the reason perhaps for our countless relapses and the feebleness of our Christian obedience to be found precisely in the fact that we are living on self-forgiveness and not a real forgiveness? Self-forgiveness can never lead to a breach with sin; this can be accomplished only by the judging and pardoning Word of God itself.

—DIETRICH BONHOEFFER

"Furthermore, we have seen with our own eyes and now testify that the Father sent his Son to be the Savior of the world. All who confess that Jesus is the Son of God have God living in them, and they live in God. We know how much God loves us, and we have put our trust in his love. God is love, and all who live in love live in God, and God lives in them."

—1 JOHN 4:14-16 (NLT)

The Big Idea: Confession gives us certainty in God's unlimited compassion, teaching us that we will *always* be able to *"approach the throne of grace with confidence, so that we may receive mercy and find grace to help us in our time of need"* (Hebrews 4:16 NIV). In this certainty, we can know we are still loved and accepted by God; we can know our talents and skills will still be used by God; we can be confident that God is with us always, even unto the ends of the earth, even in everything (Philippians 4:13).

—∿∿—

Confessing to one another keeps us honest before God. In faith, we tell another about our sins, revealing we are serious when we say we seek forgiveness and serious when we say we want to change. And through the one to whom we confess, God gives us certainty that we are forgiven because our brother or sister speaks on behalf of Jesus. We no longer face temptation alone because, Bonhoeffer says, we experience "the presence of God in the reality of the other person."

Our confessions must be specific, not general, because admitting to concrete sin helps to develop the faithful certainty that God forgives us. A general confession undermines the certainty God wants us to have when we seek forgiveness, and it also allows us to retain some small strand of pride that suggests our sin wasn't all that bad.

Jesus dealt with specific sins confessed by people who came to him knowing they needed forgiveness. And his forgiveness was relentlessly specific in that it cleansed every last bit of the sin in their lives. Bonhoeffer suggests we repeatedly do self-examination, using the Ten Commandments, to assess if we've allowed sin to slip into our lives.

Bonhoeffer notes that confession is not a law, but "an offer of divine help for the sinner." It is a gift and a blessing from God given to us as a way back to the narrow path that leads to the narrow gate, where we are once again walking in an obedient trust of Jesus. Bonhoeffer wonders who can refuse this help when God deemed it necessary to offer.

Jesus is . . .

Jesus was absolutely certain that the Father could be trusted.

To be like Jesus . . .

We must learn to trust in Jesus, who guarantees that we can *"come boldly to the throne of our gracious God"* (Hebrews 4:16 NLT).

Scripture:

"So let us come boldly to the throne of our gracious God. There we will receive his mercy, and we will find grace to help us when we need it most." Hebrews 4:16 (NLT)

Questions:

What does Paul mean when he says we can approach the throne of grace boldly? How does confessing our sins give us certainty about the love of God?

CHAPTER 34

CONFESSION: TO WHOM DO WE CONFESS?

Anybody who lives beneath the Cross and who has discerned in the Cross of Jesus the utter wickedness of all men and of his own heart will find there is no sin that can ever be alien to him. Anybody who has once been horrified by the dreadfulness of his own sin that nailed Jesus to the Cross will no longer be horrified by even the rankest sins of a brother.

—DIETRICH BONHOEFFER

"Live creatively, friends. If someone falls into sin, forgivingly restore him, saving your critical comments for yourself. You might be needing forgiveness before the day's out."

—GALATIANS 6:1 (MSG)

The Big Idea: Only those who live under the cross of Jesus can hear confession. And only those who confess can hear the confession of others.

—⁓⁓—

"It is not experience of life but experience of the Cross that makes one a worthy hearer of confessions," says Bonhoeffer. "The most experienced psychologist or observer of human nature knows infinitely less of the human heart than the simplest Christian who lives beneath the Cross of Jesus." He adds, "The greatest psychological insight, ability, and experience cannot grasp this one thing: what sin is."

The world's wisdom may know about weakness and failure, but it does not know or understand human depravity, the evil found in the godless heart. "For the message about Christ's death on the cross is nonsense to those who are being lost; but for us who are being saved it is God's power. The scripture says, *I will destroy the wisdom of the wise and set aside the understanding of the scholars*" (1 Corinthians 1:18-19 TEV). So when we confess, Bonhoeffer notes, we're not saying we're sick; rather, we're admitting we are sinners. We confess because we long to be with God, not because we want an explanation or a theory for our behavior.

Confessing to one another helps us see each other under the cross of Jesus, where we are judged, yet granted mercy through the blood of Jesus Christ. And so, Bonhoeffer says, "it is not lack of psychological knowledge but lack of love for the crucified Jesus Christ that makes us so poor and inefficient in brotherly confession."

The cross pushes us past our harsh human criticism and weak indulgences toward "the spirit of divine severity and divine love." We enter into the reality of grace—that we need God's grace because of our sin—and in that reality we see the death of our sin.

We are able to hear the confessions of others because, like King David, we confess: *"I recognize my faults; I am always conscious of my sins. I have sinned against you—only against you—and done what you consider evil. So you are right in judging me; you are justified in condemning me"* (Psalm 51:3-4 TEV).

But, also like King David, we know the joy that comes from confession, the joy of brokenness before God: *"Let me hear the sounds of joy and gladness; and though you have crushed me and broken me, I will be happy once again"* (Psalm 51:8 TEV).

We hear confession from one another so that each of us in the fellowship can experience this new gladness: *"Give me again the joy that comes from your salvation, and make me willing to obey you. Then I will teach sinners your commands, and they will turn back to you"* (Psalm 51:12-13 TEV).

Jesus is . . .

Jesus was humbled and broken before the Father.

To be like Jesus . . .

We must be broken and humbled before the Father in order to hear the confessions of others. *"My sacrifice is a humble spirit, O God; you will not reject a humble and repentant heart"* (Psalm 51:17 TEV).

Scripture:

"Create a pure heart in me, O God, and put a new and loyal spirit in me. Do not banish me from your presence; do not take your holy spirit away from me. Give me again the joy that comes from your salvation, and make me willing to obey you. Then I will teach sinners your commands, and they will turn back to you." Psalm 51:10-13 (TEV)

Questions:

God says he does not want sacrifices; instead, he wants a humble heart. What does that mean? What are the kinds of "sacrifices" we try to make before God in order to make up for our sins?

CHAPTER 35

CONFESSION: TWO DANGERS TO AVOID

Only the person who has so humbled himself can hear a
brother's confession without harm.

—Dietrich Bonhoeffer

*"But if we live in the light—just as he is in the light—then we
have fellowship with one another, and the blood of Jesus, his
Son, purifies us from every sin."*

—1 John 1:7 (tev)

The Big Idea: We're not qualified to hear the confessions of
others because of some special insight or training or unique spiritual standing on our part. We're qualified to hear each other's confessions because we are sinners who know sin and its destructive
power, and we now know Jesus and his redemptive power.

Bonhoeffer says there are two dangers to watch for as our community practices biblical confession.

First, we should never designate one person as the only person to hear confessions. Confession isn't about setting up some special, spiritual leader who acts as a mediator between God and us. Jesus is already our mediator and he paid a bloody price so that we could have a direct and intimate relationship with the Father.

Jesus gives, every believer the authority to hear another believer's confession and so Bonhoeffer teaches it is okay for you to be accountable to one person while I am accountable to another.

Second, we should guard against turning confession into a pious work. In other words, we don't confess to impress. We don't confess in order to appear spiritual.

Jesus spoke about two men who went up to the Temple to pray. One was a Pharisee and the other a tax collector. *"The Pharisee posed and prayed like this: 'Oh, God, I thank you that I am not like other people—robbers, crooks, adulterers, or, heaven forbid, like this tax man. I fast twice a week and tithe on all my income.' Meanwhile the tax man, slumped in the shadows, his face in his hands, not daring to look up, said, 'God, give mercy. Forgive me, a sinner'"* (Luke 18:11-13 MSG).

Jesus said the *"tax man, not the other, went home made right with God. If you walk around with your nose in the air, you're going to end up flat on your face, but if you're content to be simply yourself, you will become more than yourself"* (Luke 18:14 MSG).

Bonhoeffer says we confess our sins because we rely on God's promise to forgive our sin: "The forgiveness of sins is the sole ground and goal of confession." The Bible says, *"If we confess our sins to God, he will keep his promise and do what is right: he will forgive us our sins and purify us from all our wrongdoing. If we say that we have not sinned, we make a liar out of God, and his word is not in us"* (1 John 1:9-10 TEV).

Jesus is . . .

The blood of Jesus purifies us from every sin and brings us into fellowship with him.

To be like Jesus . . .

Because we are in fellowship with Jesus, we are authorized to help bring one another into the light, where God purifies us from our wrongdoing and where we can "have fellowship with one another."

Scripture:

"If, then, we say that we have fellowship with him, yet at the same time live in the darkness, we are lying both in our words and in our actions. But if we live in the light—just as he is in the light—then we have fellowship with one another, and the blood of Jesus, his Son, purifies us from every sin. ... If we say that we have not sinned, we make a liar out of God, and his word is not in us." 1 John 1:6-8, 10 (TEV)

Questions:

How can we turn confession into pious work? Why does our confession lead to certainty that God will fulfill his promises?

CHAPTER 36

THE MINISTRY OF COMMUNION

It is the command of Jesus that none should come to the altar with a heart that is unreconciled to his brother. If this command of Jesus applies to every service of worship, indeed, to every prayer we utter, then it most certainly applies to reception of the Lord's Supper.

—DIETRICH BONHOEFFER

"Perfect Love desires communion, the sharing of life together, so it cannot be expressed from a distance. God came in human form to make His love visible. God so loved the world that He came up-close in Christ."

—1 JOHN 1:1-3 (MSG)

The Big Idea: Communion is about the sharing of life. It is about knowing others and being known by others, about caring and being cared for on a deep and personal level. And, when we take Communion (the Lord's Supper) together, we should reflect the life we share with one another because the Life of Christ is active in our hearts.

We cannot love like Jesus loves us unless we enter each other's lives in an intimate and personal way. And so Jesus expects us to come up-close to each other. At the Last Supper, he spoke of the deep communion we should have with him and with one another. This is when he tells us, *"I am the vine, and you are the branches. Those who remain in me, and I in them, will bear much fruit; for you can do nothing without me"* (John 15:5 TEV).

He tells us that we must love one another, *deeply*, saying, *"I love you just as the Father loves me; remain in my love."* Then he says, *"My commandment is this: love one another, just as I love you."* Finally, he adds, *"This, then, is what I command you: love one another"* (John John 15: 9, 12, 17, TEV).

During the Last Supper, Jesus emphasizes the reality of our oneness with him, with the Father, and with each other; yet, we've lost that emphasis in the way we share the Lord's Supper today. We've reduced it to a superficial ritual, where we focus entirely on the sacrifice of Jesus, but to the exclusion of the oneness we are called to with each other.

Don't misunderstand—the death and resurrection of Jesus is the unimpeachable core of our relationship with God and each other. It is the very thing, the only thing, that brings us into communion with the Father, Son, and Holy Spirit: *"But now, in union with Christ Jesus you, who used to be far away, have been brought near by the blood of Christ"* (Ephesians 2:13 TEV).

And so our communion with Christ should compel us into communion with each other. Not in the lesser sense of communion—when we say that someone communes with nature—but in a deep, unconditional commitment to each other. Do you get that sense, do you hear that message, when you take part in communion today?

Jesus spent most of the Last Supper speaking about his love for us, and our oneness with him and the Father. He says to the Father: *"I pray that they may all be one. Father! May they be in us, just as you are in me and I am in you. May they be one, so that the world will believe that you sent me. I gave them the same glory you gave me, so that they may be one, just as you and I are one: I in them and you in me, so that they may be completely one, in order that the world may know that you sent me and that you love them as you love me"* (John 17:21-23 TEV).

Yet, somehow we've truncated the message into a memorial service for Jesus. We say, "Let's remember what he did for us," but then we stop before we get to the part where we're supposed to remember what we should do for each other because we are in union with Christ.

Jesus says our communion with each other, our love for one another, should go as far as it can possibly go: *"The greatest love you can have for your friends is to give your life for them"* (John 15:13 TEV).

Bonhoeffer says we should prepare for Communion (the Lord's Supper) in the same way we prepare for worship because Communion is worship. We prepare by slowing down, turning our eyes away from ourselves, and contemplating the infinite things God has done for us.

Jesus says, before we come to worship, we should first come to confession, re-establishing our communion with one another before we engage in worshipful communion with God: *"If you enter your place of worship and, about to make an offering, you suddenly remember a grudge a friend has against you, abandon your offering, leave immediately, go to this friend and make things right. Then and only then, come back and work things out with God"* (Matthew 5:23b-24 MSG).

Confession leads to communion and that means the day of the Lord's Supper should be "an occasion of joy for the Christian community" because we have re-established the unity between us, confident in God's promises that we will receive "forgiveness, new life, and salvation."

Jesus is . . .

Through his blood, Jesus brings us into communion with God and with one another (Ephesians 2:13).

To be like Jesus . . .

When we are united *in Christ*, we *"can join together with one voice, giving praise and glory to God . . ."* (Romans 15:6 NLT).

Scripture:

"Perfect Love desires communion, the sharing of life together, so it cannot be expressed from a distance. God came in human form to make His love visible. God so loved the world that He came up-close in Christ." 1 John 1:1-3 (MSG)

Questions:

Bonhoeffer notes that Jesus was accused of blasphemy for forgiving sinners. What do your attitudes and actions reveal about your thoughts on forgiving sinners? Do you agree we are all sinners wholly and totally dependent upon Jesus; what do your attitudes and actions say? Do you think there are some sinners who are worse than you; what would Jesus say about that? Do you have any broken relationships that need to be repaired before you enter worship? If yes, what are you going to do about that?